Sarah Fritschner's

H🕯LIDAYS

Menus and Recipes
for the Fall Holiday Season

BUTLER BOOKS
LOUISVILLE

Published by Butler Books
P.O. Box 7311
Louisville, KY 40207

Printed in USA by Hamilton Printing, Louisville, KY

To my neighbors:
It takes a village, guys. Thanks.

HOLIDAY MENUS

INTRODUCTION

The six or so weeks that we often call "the holidays" are anything but for those of us who prepare by shopping, cooking, decorating, partying, entertaining, cleaning, wrapping and visiting, in addition to what we already consider a busy life.

In spite of ourselves, we love it.

At our house, festivities start early, as relatives begin arriving the Wednesday before Thanksgiving. A full 17 people finally gather around the dining room table for the Thanksgiving meal; most of them will be spending three days and nights with us.

Everyone has jobs to do for Thanksgiving. One sister-in-law manages the turkey, another decorates the dining room and the table with fall color. My husband irons the linen tablecloth and napkins. One brother makes cranberry sauce; he and his wife manage clean-up. Another brother runs back and forth next door, where we have full access to the neighbors' oven and fridge—they go out for the day. He also buys the Krispy Kremes that morning.

And so, with help, I manage to pull off feeding a house full of people.

Having the aid of others does help. So does a tradition. With the rituals of the holidays come the expectations of the menu—food that must never change, and the dishes that can.

For us, Thanksgiving dinner must have homemade yeast rolls. Turkey, cranberry sauce and dressing always appear. Our desserts are different from most households, but seem to suit us—chocolate cream pie and cherry pie. And one tradition we always observe: there is never, ever enough gravy.

While all these foods take time to prepare, tradition, routine, and planning help take the stress away from a hectic time. That leaves us up for the fun of visiting, camaraderie, sharing, and giving.

There are many ways to entertain during this six-week period and every family has, or makes, its own traditions. One friend has an open house on New Year's Day, another hosts a cookie exchange party. For years we've had a neighbor party in early December, and neighbors bring gifts for children in need—typically hat and glove sets. We all eat, drink, gossip and catch up on the latest in real estate prices.

Food retailers tell us that this is a time of hearty breakfasts. We serve more bacon, eggs, ham and syrup during these dark days. Breakfast and brunch make great parties; they don't interfere with evening plans, and they can be less expensive to give. Ditto for late-afternoon teas. It's also a time of caroling parties, tree trimming parties, cocktail buffets, lavish dinners, festive luncheons.

And so we give you a choice of menus for holiday entertaining solutions—breakfast or cocktail party, soup supper or sit-down-dinner. Though at first glance Thanksgiving might not seem to resemble Hanukkah, in truth both menus feature recipes that can serve you well during the holidays and at other times when you want to serve great food to good friends and family.

Need a memory refresher for roasting turkey? Want to try making your own dressing? Looking for a safe eggnog recipe or an easy, non-alcoholic punch?

Here we give you the plan—menu ideas for many different ways of entertaining, the advice about making the work easier or making the food ahead of time, and the time-tested, family-tested recipes that help you make food traditions to keep holidays more fun and less frantic.

Making gravy

THANKSGIVING TURKEY

Seventy-five million turkeys will be shoved into ovens this holiday season, and there will be seventy-five million cooks wondering if they couldn't have done a better job of roasting them. There are a few exceptions—cooks who have experimented with cooking methods long enough to come up with one that roasts the perfect bird. But many of us will find ourselves compensating for a dry turkey by making extra gravy. Not a bad way to spend Thanksgiving, of course, but a turkey doesn't need to be overcooked.

Most families roast a turkey only once a year, so there are always questions. I'll try to build your turkey-roasting confidence by answering some of the questions here and give basic roasting instructions. Further on, you'll find information about brining, frying, and smoking turkey.

Turkey issues

In general (some of the exceptions follow) all turkeys—and turkey breasts —roast at 325 degrees. Time is the only variable. Use a per-pound chart to help you plan the timing of your other dinner dishes, but for perfectly cooked meat, you'll need a meat thermometer.

• **Using a meat thermometer**: I find meat thermometers more reliable than pop-up plastic timers that come in the turkey, especially if I'm roasting a fresh bird. Usually pop-up timers tell you one thing: your bird is overcooked.

A smaller bird takes more time to cook per pound than a larger bird, because muscle transfers the heat more efficiently than bone. As a result, a 12-pound bird needs more minutes per pound than an 18-pound bird, so you can see that the minutes-per-pound cooking method has its limitations.

If you use a traditional thermometer that goes into the oven with the bird, place it in the thickest part of the thigh, not touching the bone. If you use an instant-read thermometer, remove the meat from the oven before you test the temperature, either in the thigh or in the thickest part of the breast. The meat should register 170 degrees. (All meat is safe after 165 degrees; experts recommend higher temperatures for palatability.)

• **Bird in a bag**: Many fans exult the cooking of turkey in an oven-roasting bag. It becomes fall-from-the-bone tender. The skin also remains very moist and the joints are loose and flimsy, so the bird falls apart easily after it's cooked. You won't get the golden, crunchy skin many people associate with the Norman Rockwell turkey. If the idea of a soft, braised meat appeals to you, follow the directions for roasting that comes with the bags you buy.

• **To roast in the oven**: Place the bird, breast up, on a rack in a shallow pan no more than two inches deep. Deeper pans will impede browning meat and tend to stew the bottom. Avoid using the deep, disposable aluminum pans sold in the supermarket. If I had a dollar for every story I've heard about the pan twisting and splashing hot fat/turkey drippings I could pay the deductible at an immediate care clinic.

• **Don't worry about basting**: it doesn't make the meat juicier. Opening the door periodically to baste lengthens the cooking time, which dries out the meat. Basting can give the bird an even color, however. It's really your call.

Before roasting the turkey, salt and pepper to taste, and brush oil or melted butter over the skin. It'll brown more evenly if you brush it with a little fat before roasting.

• **Don't stuff the meat**: Stuffing the bird guarantees overcooked meat. To get the stuffing to a safe 165 degrees requires overcooking the breast meat. Put an onion, a piece of celery and some herbs inside the cavity to add flavor to the pan juices.

• **For easier carving**: Allow the turkey to stand for 15 or 20 minutes. Tip the bird to pour the juices out of the cavity of the bird, then transfer it to the serving platter. Use the pan juices to make the gravy.

It's safe to eat a turkey that has been frozen since last year. If it has been stored in the deep freeze (not the refrigerator freezer), it's good for up to two years, and safe after that. If the turkey has been frozen at warmer than 0 degrees, it might have freezer burn or be dried out. But it should still be safe.

To keep turkey leftovers, refrigerate them within two hours of being removed from the oven. Turkey leftovers, stuffing and gravy can be kept 3 days in the refrigerator, according to turkey experts. Frugal family managers will tell you they keep longer than that, but you're pushing it at five days.

• **Freezing leftovers**: If you're pretty sure you can't finish all the leftovers in three days, go ahead and freeze them. Freeze them in portions you'll use—say, a pound wrapped in foil or in a freezer container. Dressing also freezes beautifully (even if it contains an egg). Leftovers will keep in fairly good condition for six months. After that they lose their luster (but are still safe to eat). If you're thawing gravy, expect it to thin considerably.

   • **Planning how much to buy**: Turkey experts tell us to buy a pound of turkey per person at our Thanksgiving table—that is, if you're feeding 12 people, buy a 12-pound turkey. That much allows for the waste of bones and for leftovers. The bigger turkey you buy, the more meat you'll have per bones, that is, a greater yield of meat you'll get off the bird.

   • **Plan ahead for roasting**: Before you roast, you probably need to thaw. Refrigerator thawing is the safest and yields the tastiest meat (the bird doesn't lose so much juice). Plan on one day in the refrigerator for every 5 pounds of turkey, then throw in an extra day for good measure. If you must thaw at the last minute, submerge the bird in a sink of cold water; allow 30 minutes per pound for thawing. Change water every 30 minutes to keep it cool enough to prevent bacterial growth.

APPROXIMATE ROASTING TIMES
Roast at 325 degrees on shallow racks in 2-inch-deep open pans.

NET WEIGHT UNSTUFFED

9 to 12 lbs.	3 to 3 1/2 hours
12 to 16 lbs.	3 1/2 to 4 hours
16 to 20 lbs.	4 to 4 1/2 hours
20 to 24 lbs.	4 1/2 to 5 hours

NET WEIGHT STUFFED

9 to 12 lbs.	3 1/2 to 4 hours
12 to 16 lbs.	4 to 4 1/2 hours
16 to 20 lbs.	4 1/2 to 5 hours
20 to 24 lbs.	5 to 6 hours

ROAST TURKEY

My extended family gathers each year for Thanksgiving and my sister-in-law cooks the turkey. Her father's family was Italian, so she's grown up rubbing the turkey with olive oil.

One 18-pound turkey, thawed if previously frozen
1/2 cup melted butter or olive oil
Salt and pepper
1 rib celery, optional
1 onion, optional

Lower your oven rack to the next-to-lowest level before you heat the oven. Heat oven to 325 degrees.

Remove the giblets from cavities in the turkey. There's a large cavity and a small one at opposite ends. Check them both and remove the giblets and neck. Set aside to use in "cooking giblets."

Rinse the turkey and dry it well. Place the wing tips "akimbo"— that is, tuck them firmly underneath the turkey, so the middle wing joint juts out at 90 degrees. Brush the turkey all over with melted butter or olive oil. If the bird is not "prebasted," sprinkle it liberally with salt. Grind or sprinkle pepper all over. Cut the celery and onion in 2 or 3 pieces and place inside the large cavity. Tuck a piece of aluminum foil tightly over the breast for the first hour of cooking. The foil "tent" deflects the heat from the breast, allowing the dark meat to cook a little faster, so the two different types of meat cook more evenly.

Place the turkey on a rack in a sturdy, shallow, roasting pan. Add 1 cup giblet broth or water. Place turkey in the oven and allow it to bake 1

hour. Remove foil. Continue to cook according to time chart or until the thermometer registers 170 degrees in the breast.

What's a giblet? Giblets are the extras that likely come with your turkey—the heart, liver, gizzard and neck.

The liver is the dark, flattish giblet. If you are a clever or industrious cook you will make something with it. You might combine it with pork or duck to make paté. Check your French cookbooks for such a recipe.

Cooking giblets: Place neck, gizzard and heart in 2 quarts of water and bring to a boil. The heart and gizzard are springy and firm to the touch. If you've cut any flaps or pieces from the turkey, put those in the water also, along with the turkey neck. If you like the flavor of liver, you may add the liver the last 5 minutes of cooking. Otherwise, discard liver. Let the giblets simmer, uncovered, 1 hour.

Strain and let the liquid cool. Remove any meat you can from the neck, mince the gizzard and heart. You can add these pieces to the gravy or to your bread dressing, making "giblet gravy" or "giblet dressing." Save the giblet broth to use as the liquid in gravy, dressing, mashed potatoes or soup.

GRAVY WITHOUT LUMPS

The overriding concern of a gravy cook is to make it lump-free. But there are other concerns as well. You want a flavorful gravy, and one that's not too thin or thick. Gravy may have been the second thing I learned to cook—after oatmeal cookies. I stood on a chair to make it—I remember that much—and I did it with a metal spoon. (A whisk would not grace my kitchen for another 20 years.) I make it the same way today, without having to stand on a chair.

Remove the cooked turkey from the roasting rack, and the rack from the roasting pan. Pour residual drippings into a large glass measuring cup or other container. If it's in a glass measuring cup, you can see the clearish fat rise to the top, and the darker brown drippings settle to the bottom. Use those drippings in your stuffing or in your gravy (or both). You'll need the fat to start your gravy.

Leave all the brown stuff stuck to the bottom of the pan. Place the pan lengthwise over two burners on lowest heat.

Equal amounts of fat and flour are stirred into the pan. (The proportion of ingredients—always estimated—is 2 tablespoons each of fat and flour to 1 cup of liquid.)

Broccoli with Lemon Sauce (page 131)

Bourbon Balls (page 91)

Champagne Punch (page 141) and Spicy Almonds (page 141)

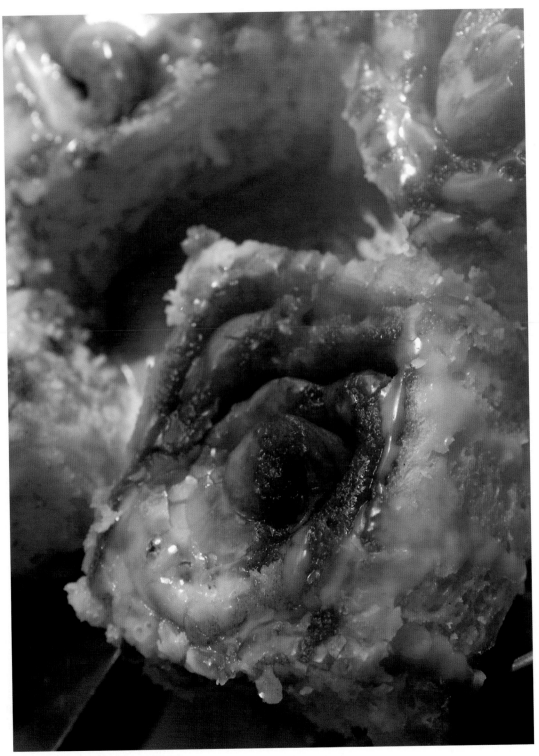

Cinnamon Rolls (page 102)

Cheese Herb Frittata (page 101) and Sour Cream Coffee Cake (page 105)

Kale Stew (page 154)

Turkey Fried Rice (page 59)

Lemon Honey Salmon (page 112) and Cauliflower with Bread Crumbs (page 116)

Mashed Potatoes (page 38)

Sweet Potato Casserole (page 40)

Mussels Vinaigrette (page 147)

Peppermint Brownies (page 93)

Pumpkin Pie (page 42) and Chocolate Cream Pie (page 44)

Spice-Rubbed Beef Roast (page 67) and Sweet and Sour Green Beans (page 68)

Chocolate Chocolate Chip Cookies (page 88)

Anise Almond Biscotti (page 89)

Thumbprints (page 87)

Tomato–Artichoke Soup (page 75) and Very Best White Bread (page 72)

Cornbread Dressing (page 32)

Tiramisu (page 158)

Tuxedo Cakes (page 148)

TURKEY GRAVY

1/2 cup turkey fat from drippings
1/2 cup all-purpose flour
1 teaspoon salt
1 teaspoon (freshly ground) pepper
4 cups drippings (without fat), giblet broth, canned chicken broth
   or water

Add fat to the pan over low heat. Sprinkle in flour and stir well to combine completely. Add salt and pepper and stir to combine. Add the liquid gradually and stir with a whisk, if you have one. A spoon will work, but a whisk works better to break up lumps and keep the mixture smooth. All of these precautions help prevent lumping when you add the liquid. The mixture will seize up and get quite stiff as you add liquid. Keep adding liquid, a little at a time, and keep stirring, and the gravy begins to loosen and resemble a sauce.

Allow the gravy to come to a boil. The gravy will thicken upon standing, so it is wise to make it a little thinner in the pan, ensuring that by the time it comes to the table it will be perfect. Taste before serving and add salt and pepper if your gravy seems bland.

This makes about 4 cups, which is what I would call a good start. You may want to double or triple this recipe, if your large family uses gravy on turkey, potatoes and dressing and you want some tomorrow. If you need extra fat, use butter.

BRINED TURKEY

One of the best turkeys I've ever cooked has been following directions of an old *Cook's Illustrated* magazine. The combination of brining and hot, fast cooking yields a turkey that is exceptionally moist in a very short time. I don't brine turkey any more, because my sister-in-law is in charge of cooking the turkey at Thanksgiving and she doesn't brine it. And certainly the one turkey that's better than a brined one is one you didn't have to cook yourself.

There's a lot of fussing with a brined turkey. But if you'd like to try it out, we bring you a great technique. This method can be used on an 18-pound turkey, but bigger birds are pretty difficult to wield once they're hot. If you want more meat, consider using two smaller birds rather than one larger one.

1 12- to 14-pound turkey, rinsed thoroughly, giblets, neck removed
2 cups salt
2 medium onions, chopped coarsely
1 medium carrot, chopped coarsely
1 celery rib, chopped coarsely
1 teaspoon dried thyme
1/2 cup butter, melted

Remove giblets and prepare as described in Cooking Giblets on page 15.

Place turkey in a non-reactive (stainless steel, plastic, ceramic, etc.) pot or container large enough to hold it. Pour salt into neck and body cavities; pour salt all over turkey and rub into its skin. Add cold water to

cover, rubbing the bird and stirring water until salt dissolves. Set turkey in refrigerator or other cool location (in our location, that could mean the deck or the garage) for at least 4 hours or overnight.

When ready to cook, remove turkey from salt water and rinse it all over for several minutes so that all traces of salt water are gone. Discard water. Heat oven to 400 degrees. Prepare vegetables. Put half of the vegetables and thyme in the large cavity of the turkey. Bring turkey legs together by trussing, simply tying with cotton string, or by using the little plastic or metal pieces provided to secure the legs. Scatter the remaining vegetables and herbs in the shallow roasting pan and add 1 cup of your giblet broth to the pan. Set a V-rack (on its widest setting, if it has settings) in the pan. Brush the entire breast side of the turkey with butter, and put the turkey, breast side down, on the V-rack. Brush the back of the turkey with butter. Roast for 45 minutes.

Remove pan from the oven (close oven door); use your basting brush to brush the turkey with a little more butter and some of the pan drippings. Add water to the pan at this point, or at any point, if the vegetables appear to be in danger of burning. With a wad of paper toweling in each hand (or potholders or clean cloth towels), turn the turkey so that one leg/thigh side is up. Baste a little more, then return to the oven for 15 minutes. Remove from oven, close the oven door and turn the turkey so that the other leg/thigh side is up. Baste a little more, then roast another 15 minutes. Remove turkey from oven again, baste and turn it breast side up. Roast until a meat thermometer stuck in the deepest part of the thigh registers 170 degrees, about 30 to 45 minutes.

Transfer turkey to a platter and allow it to rest 20 to 30 minutes before carving. Make gravy according to directions using pan drippings (page 16).

SMOKED TURKEY

The Pilgrims and Indians couldn't depend on their trusty GE convertible conventional/convection oven to help them prepare the dinner that schoolchildren now call the First Thanksgiving. Cooks have been using wood and charcoal to get their turkey to the table for centuries. The farther you travel below the Mason-Dixon line, the more sense it makes to smoke turkeys. It's no problem to hang out on the patio checking the status of your bird on a sunny, breezy day in the mid-70s.

But the ultimate reason for smoking a turkey is the taste. From first bite of drumstick to the last bit of broth simmered from the bones, a smoked turkey has no peer when it comes to adding flavor to the holiday meal. It smells great, it looks beautiful and it tastes outstanding. Which is why I've been known to be checking the embers at 3 a.m. on a windy 20-degree night. For some, weather is less a deterrent than the imprecision of the process. There's no set of instructions, no recipe that can prepare you for the decisions you'll have to make. Though most cooking is a mix of art and science, smoking meat is nearly all art. There are so many variables—the outdoor temperature, the quality and quantity of the coals, even the wind-chill factor can affect how long smoking takes. So do the size of the turkey and the initial starting temperature of the meat (a room-temperature turkey takes less time than a straight-from-the-refrigerator bird). Restoking coals might cause you to increase smoking time, or not, depending on the type of smoker you have. Your smoking process might be a combination of grilling and smoking, which requires a set of skills that a water-smoker wouldn't require. June Cleaver would not love smoking a bird. You can't really do it wearing heels and pearls; some smokers are designed so that you must get on your knees to check the status of the coals and the water.

Without breaking the world into odious stereotypical gender roles,

let's just say that smoking a turkey is a project that might prove interesting to people who would otherwise spend all day watching football. Furthermore, although smoking is imprecise and a little cumbersome, it is absolutely forgiving. A turkey that needs to smoke in a water smoker for 12 hours can go 14, 16, even 18 hours and emerge juicy and flavorful; in short, perfect food for dinner. As long as you cook it long enough, it's almost impossible to ruin. Smoking a turkey outdoors leaves the counters, oven and stove free. You have lots of room to move and no last-minute panic about how to get everything to the table at once. Your vegetables can be heating in the oven while the turkey stays warm out on the patio. Plus, smoking turkey can be interesting and fun.

A 12-pound bird is about the biggest turkey you'll probably want to smoke. I smoked a 20-pounder once, starting the fire at 10:30 one night, then getting up at 4 a.m. to start a new round of coals, restoke the fire and add fresh smoking chips. It was fun, but only once, and it wouldn't be fun before having 20 people to my house for a huge dinner I have to clean up after. Keep the smoker on a brick patio, cement sidewalk or other non-flammable surface. Hot charcoal or chips will inevitably find their way onto the ground. If you're outside where there might be leaves and sticks, you might want to hose down the area; keeping the surroundings damp makes you more confident when you walk away to catch the second half of the game. Save all leftovers, bones, fat, cartilage and meat to make into broth. Nothing tastes better than broth from smoked meat. You can cook rice in it, or make bean soup or vegetable soup, or use it in stir-fries, etc. Make the broth from scraps when you collect them, then you can freeze it for later. If you're buying a new smoker, it will come with an owner's manual that will get you started.

Charcoal is different from smoking chips, but both are available at

continued

most supermarkets. Smoking chips are also available at some hardware stores and specialty cooking-supply stores. They are hardwood chips, made of anything from hickory to mesquite. A little of the chips goes a long way.

Though you won't find anything in the owner's manual about gloves, I can't imagine smoking meat without adequate covering for my hands. There are too many times you need to handle hot racks, or charcoal or pans of water. Potholders will be unwieldy and even oven gloves wouldn't be suitable for handling water pans—hot water would too readily soak through.

SMOKING A TURKEY

• **In a water smoker**: Drain and rinse thawed turkey. Remove giblets from body cavities and follow directions for cooking giblets (page 15). Pat the turkey dry. Remove lid, rack and pans from the cylindrical cooking chamber. Open the vents on the side. Fill the charcoal pan (the deep one that goes on the bottom of the chamber) with about 10 pounds of charcoal. Soak the charcoal with about 1 cup of charcoal-lighter fluid, letting it soak in about 5 minutes (do not use instant-lighting charcoal). Place the charcoal inside the cooking chamber, light it and let it burn about 30 minutes, or until covered with a gray ash.

Line water pan with aluminum foil (to make cleaning easier). Position the pan on the middle level of the cooking chamber. Fill it with hot water to speed up cooking, or tap water if time is more flexible.

Place rack on top of cooking chamber and place turkey on rack, breast-side up. If you have a regular meat thermometer (instead of an instant-read type), insert the thermometer into the thickest part of thigh (even if your smoker has a thermometer indicating the inside heat of the

unit, you will also need to know the internal temperature of the meat). Cover turkey with lid and close vents, if any. If you would like to add hardwood chunks, soak two hefty handfuls of them for 30 to 90 minutes in water to cover, then drain and add them to charcoal by passing them through the open vents after the charcoal has burned about 1 1/2 hours. If your smoker has no vent, place the soaked and drained hardwood on the hot, gray charcoal before putting the water pan in place. If your smoker has side vents, insert a dozen or so briquettes every 1 1/2 hours or so. If your smoker has no side vents, preheat about 5 pounds of coals so they get covered with gray ash (do this in your conventional grill, or in a chimney starter, or in another flame-proof container that seems suitable). Disassemble the water smoker, by lifting the turkey out, then lifting out the water tray, then the tray of spent coals. Dump the spent coals in a suitable place (where they won't start a fire), then refill the smoker tray with new coals. Re-assemble the smoker and continue to smoke the turkey until its internal temperature is 170 degrees.

The internal temperature of the smoker should be about 250 degrees. Cooking time varies (even a cool windy day can increase the necessary cooking time). As a guide, an 8- to 12-pound turkey will take 4 to 8 hours, and a 12- to 18-pound turkey will take 6 to 10 hours. If you err, cook it longer rather than shorter. A smoked turkey will be very forgiving if you overcook it, tending to remain juicy and flavorful even if smoked several hours longer than absolutely required. In a pinch, take the turkey out of the smoker and finish it in the oven. Let the turkey stand 15 minutes before carving.

• **In a kettle grill**: Drain and rinse thawed turkey. Remove giblets from body cavity and follow directions in cooking giblets (page 15). Pat the turkey dry. Remove cooking rack from grill. Fill one-half of the bottom

continued

of the grill with charcoal (up to 10 pounds if you can). Open vents under charcoal.Place a foil pan (or make a foil pan from sheet aluminum) on the other side of the grill. Soak the charcoal with charcoal-lighter fluid (about 1/2 cup in all) and let rest five minutes. Light the coals and when they are covered with a gray ash, fill the foil pan with water (a watering can is handy for this). Replace cooking rack. Put turkey on the rack over water-filled drip pan. Cover with lid, positioning top vent over turkey (you want to draw smoke from the charcoal across the grill and around the turkey). Once the turkey has cooked an hour, you may want to put soaked hardwood chips on the burning charcoal to add a smokier flavor to the bird. Soak about two handfuls of chips for 30 to 90 minutes. Drain well and place on top of the burning charcoal. The turkey is done when it registers about 170 degrees in the thigh. The interior heat of the grill should be about 350 degrees, but it's difficult to tell for sure, since an oven thermometer in the grill will be covered in carbon after not too long in the chamber. A meat thermometer is critical to proper cooking. Plan on 11 to 15 minutes per pound (it takes less time to roast the bird in the kettle grill than it does to smoke it in a water smoker).

FRIED TURKEY

The deep-fried turkey is a Southern specialty. Only in the South is it warm enough to stand outside during game season; only in Louisiana, South Carolina and other parts of the Deep South can you plan on cooking Thanksgiving dinner outdoors. And it's outdoors where you must fry the bird, most easily using a three-legged camp stove with a butane feeder that produces high heat. The gear you'll need: a camp stove, a pot deep enough to hold 5 gallons of peanut oil and a turkey, and a metal stand that goes in the pot to keep the turkey upright and helps it drain when you lift it out. It also helps to have a thermometer with a long stem to test the fat.

It's essential that an extra-large pot is used to cook the bird. Five gallons of peanut oil take up a lot of room, the turkey displaces a lot of oil, and the oil boils violently as the juice from the turkey hits the hot oil and begins to bubble and steam.

This is not a chore to be done where there are lots of little children running around. Five gallons of 325-degree oil is dangerous. Though the turkey takes only minutes to cook—3 to 3 1/2 minutes per pound, actually—the fat takes awhile to heat up. This fat-heating is less of a factor if you're cooking multiple turkeys, but is a bigger percentage of your day if you're only cooking one turkey. On a 50-degree day, allow at least 45 minutes for your fat to heat up. Keep an extra-long thermometer around to keep tabs on the fat. Constant temperature is one of the cardinal rules of deep-frying. Frying the bird at 300 to 325 degrees means it must be 350 when the meat goes in.

Frying fresh turkey has advantages; it tends not to spit and churn the fat as much as one that has been frozen. Both frozen and fresh birds must be patted dry to avoid the problem of hot fat boiling over. Rubbing the turkey with spices and aromatics is common practice among turkey fryers; injecting them with flavorful liquid is another. I've heard conflicting opinions about whether these seasoning methods are worth the trouble. Once the turkey is rubbed and the oil has reached the proper temperature (the proper temperature is a matter of opinion), the turkey is lowered into the grease and timing begins. Figure time between 3 minutes per pound (42 minutes for a 14-pound bird) and 3 1/2 minutes (49 minutes) to estimate minimum and maximum cooking time. These turkeys cook in a fraction of the time that a roasted turkey takes. Perhaps that's why the turkey tastes so much better than a roasted turkey. It's much juicier and not at all greasy. The most important rule for successful deep-frying is this: Keep the oil clean and the temperature constant.

continued

Other tips:

• Use vegetable oil that has not been hydrogenated and that has no preservatives. Vegetable oil has a higher smoke point than fats that have been hydrogenated or that have added preservatives.

• Choose a pot that is larger than the heat source. A pot bigger than its heat source will allow flammable oil to spit wide of the flame.

• Use pans that are deeper than they are wide. Wide surface area on pots allows more oil to oxidize, which causes faster breakdown.

• Never fill the pot more than half full of oil. You'll need at least 3 inches between the surface of the oil and the top of the pot to allow room for the oil to bubble up when the food is added.

• Keep an eye on the temperature. Turkey-frying contraptions usually come with a long-stemmed thermometer that can hang on the side of the pot and reach into the oil. The thermometer should measure temperatures from 325 to 450 degrees and have a metal clamp so it can hang on the side of the pot.

• Do not put the heat source on its highest setting. You'll want leeway when the frying begins. Invest your time at the beginning preheating your oil. Then, if the temperature drops quite a bit when you put the food in, you'll have some heat you can crank on.

• If the oil begins to smoke, discard it and start with new. Smoking oil is old and will make the food taste bad. It is also more likely to combust.

• Use proper tools to lift the turkey from the oil. Spring-loaded tongs, an Oriental wire mesh skimmer and long-handled forks are useful.

A slotted spoon is not—oil often collects in them despite their slots.

• Drain foods on a wire rack or in the basket in which they were fried. Resist the temptation to put the food on an absorbent surface. The turkey will just sit in the grease.

• If you're frying other foods, keep the turkey warm by draping it with foil and putting it on a rack, in a baking pan, in an oven on low setting.

• Always allow the oil to cool before you move it. When the oil is cool enough to move, filter it into a clean pot or back into its original container. There are any number of filters you can use—try a coffee filter in a large sieve.

• Cool the oil completely before you dispose of it. Dispose of it in the large container in which it came, setting it out with the garbage.

Ricing potatoes for mashing

THANKSGIVING SIDES AND DESSERTS

Writing a chapter on Thanksgiving side dishes is a challenge because everybody has different traditions. For some, a relish tray of carrots, black and green olives and celery always starts the day. Others don't consider it Thanksgiving without gelatin salad or mincemeat pie or chestnut dressing.

Whole books could be (and have been) written about Thanksgiving. We offer you just a few traditional side dishes here. Make some of them and you will have a fabulous dinner you can be proud of.

Juggling the timing on Thanksgiving side dishes is easy for us. We use our neighbors' oven because they go out for dinner. You may not be quite so lucky.

Don't stress when trying to juggle all the recipes that tell you to bake items at different temperatures; most will perform well 50 degrees above or below what the recipe requires. If your turkey dressing recipe says to heat the dressing at 325, but your sweet potato casserole says 350, feel free to cook them both together at either temperature.

Easy Giblet Dressing
Cornbread Dressing
Crosscut Brussels Sprouts
Cooked Forever Green Beans
Cranberry Sauce
Cranberry Pear Chutney
Mashed Potatoes
Sweet Potato Casserole
Not-Too-Sweet Sesame Sweet Potatoes
Pumpkin Pie
Chocolate Pie

EASY GIBLET DRESSING

Homemade dressing is a cinch to make. It's cubes of bread—you can do that—seasoned with any one of several combinations of seasonings. We use thyme below. Sage would work. So would tarragon.

Here's the simple process. Stack 6 pieces of good-quality sandwich bread (whole wheat or white, or your choice). Use a serrated knife to cut through the stack about 1/2 inch from the edge. Slice through the bread at 1/2-inch intervals, then cut at right angles to the original slices to create cubes. Put the cubes in a bowl and let them set out overnight.

For every 6 slices of regular, supermarket-purchased bread, you will get roughly 5 cups of bread cubes. Ten cups of dressing will serve about 15 people, depending on how many side dishes you have and how much your family likes stuffing.

Health professionals say it's safest not to stuff the bird, but to bake dressing separately. Connoisseurs agree; a stuffed bird takes longer to cook and increases the chance that the breast meat will dry out. Remember, it is safe to freeze leftover dressing, even if yours has an egg in it. If you'd rather not use wine, substitute a cup of chicken or turkey broth.

3 strips bacon
1 large red or yellow onion, diced (about 2 cups)
1 cup dry white wine
1/2 teaspoon salt
1 teaspoon thyme
1/2 to 1 teaspoon (freshly ground) pepper
1/4 cup butter
10 cups fresh bread cubes, left out overnight
Chopped giblets (optional)
A little turkey stock or water

Cook bacon until crisp, in a Dutch oven or other wide, deep pan over medium-low heat. Remove from pan and add onion. Cook over medium heat, stirring occasionally, until onion begins to brown. Add wine, salt, thyme and pepper and turn heat to high. Boil wine rapidly until it has all but disappeared. Add butter. When it melts, add bread cubes and toss over medium heat to moisten and toast them. Add chopped giblets, if desired, and as much turkey stock as it takes to get the texture you like, up to 1 cup). If you add more liquid—enough to make moist dressing that can be scooped up with an ice-cream scoop—your yield will decrease quite a bit, so add more bread if you wish.

Warm through in a 350-degree oven. Serves 15. You can make this dressing a day ahead and keep it in the refrigerator.

CORNBREAD DRESSING

There's a portion of the South where households serve—or used to serve —cornbread every day, and there were plenty of leftovers. If you don't have leftovers, we give you a recipe for cornbread here. This recipe asks that you add turkey drippings from the roasting pan, but if you make the dressing ahead of time, you won't have drippings from the pan. You have several choices: you can make the dressing ahead of time and drizzle in turkey-pan drippings before you bake it, or you can make it with fat or drippings that you have frozen from other turkey/chicken roasting times, or you can, as the recipe suggests, use butter.

Cornbread:
4 tablespoons melted butter
2 1/4 cups white cornmeal
1/4 cup flour
1 1/4 teaspoon salt
1 tablespoon baking powder
1 egg
1 1/2 cups milk

Dressing:
1 recipe corn bread, broken up and lightly toasted
1/2 teaspoon dried thyme
1 cup chopped onion
1 cup chopped celery
2 eggs
1/2 teaspoon (freshly ground) black pepper
1 cup turkey stock or chicken broth
1/2 cup turkey drippings or melted butter

To make the cornbread:

Heat the oven to 450 degrees and put the butter in a 9-inch cast iron skillet or other heavy pan. Place the pan in the oven to melt the butter and heat the pan. Mix the cornmeal with flour, salt, baking powder, egg and milk. When the butter is beginning to brown, remove the skillet from the oven and tip it to coat the sides of the pan. Pour the rest in the batter and stir to mix. Pour batter into the hot pan and bake 25 minutes, or until the cornbread is golden brown around the edges. You can serve this corn bread hot as cornbread; save it a day or two at room temperature to make dressing, or freeze it to make the dressing up to 3 months later.

To make the dressing:

Crumble the cornbread into a large bowl. Add thyme, onion and celery. In a small bowl, beat eggs with pepper, then stir into cornbread. Drizzle in broth and drippings. Spoon into a 9- by 9-inch pan or similar baking dish (you may now store this in the refrigerator or freezer). When ready to bake, heat oven to 425 degrees. Bake until golden brown, 20 to 30 minutes, depending on if it is cold to begin with. Serves 10.

CROSSCUT BRUSSELS SPROUTS

Before you say "yuck" and turn the page, be aware that this recipe has converted many non-Brussels sprouts eaters.

The shape of a Brussels sprout makes it nearly impossible to cook well and certainly nobody likes a huge piece of sulfury-tasting vegetable in his or her mouth. But if you cut the sprouts vertically and cook them briefly in good-tasting fat (garlic butter or bacon fat, for instance), you have a completely different vegetable for dinner.

2 pounds Brussels sprouts
2 cloves garlic, minced (about 1 teaspoon)
1/4 cup butter, or mix butter and olive oil, or use bacon fat
Salt and freshly ground pepper

Cut Brussels sprouts vertically into slices about 1/8-inch thick (about 4 slices to each medium Brussels sprout). Place garlic and butter or oil in a wide skillet pan and heat over medium-high heat until garlic is fragrant. Add Brussels sprouts and cook, stirring occasionally, until they are bright green and tender, but firm, and some have browned. Season with salt and pepper. Serves 8.

COOKED FOREVER GREEN BEANS

A famous restaurateur leaned over to ask me at dinner one night, "Are the beans supposed to be like this?" The answer? "Yep." If you want green beans served fashionably *al dente*, check the recipe on page 68.

A ham hock
1 onion, diced
1/2 teaspoon red pepper flakes
2 pounds green beans
1 teaspoon sugar
1 teaspoon salt

Combine ham hock with onion, red pepper flakes and 1 quart water in a large pot. Bring to a boil, then simmer, uncovered, about an hour.

Wash and trim green beans. Cut the beans into 2-inch (or so) lengths and add to water along with sugar and salt. Bring to a boil, then simmer, uncovered, another hour or until nearly all the liquid is gone. Remove the ham hock from the pot and when it is cool enough to handle, remove the meat from the hock and add it back to the pot. Serves 8.

CRANBERRY SAUCE

When the Pilgrims arrived, they found berry vines creeping through the large, sandy bogs in New England. The cranberries' waxy skins allow them to last for months in cool temperatures, providing both the flavor and nutrition of fresh fruit in the dead of winter.

The instructions on a bag of cranberries will tell you to mix 2 parts (measured) cranberries with 1 part sugar and 1 part water—that is, cook 2 cups of cranberries with 1 cup sugar and 1 cup water. Boil the mixture until the berries pop (5 minutes), then cool and chill. It's a good guide, but limiting. Mix the cranberries with apple or orange juice, or add orange zest (or ground orange or chopped apple). Bring the berries to a boil, and when they pop, sweeten to taste.

Except for the occasional cranberry lover who heaps sauce upon his plate, the average cranberry eater will take small bites, as appropriate for any relish. A cook might think there's too much left over from cooking a whole bag. Don't worry: Whole cranberry sauce keeps until Christmas and beyond.

PEAR AND CRANBERRY CHUTNEY

This chutney requires more ingredients than straight cranberry sauce, but the result is more interesting, and more appealing to people who don't love straight cranberries. Adding brown sugar, apple juice, vinegar, ginger and orange to this dish tones down the natural bitterness in the berries. Dried fruit makes a strong statement. Prepare this chutney two days or two weeks in advance. It is a good keeper, and also good on poultry sandwiches.

1 tablespoon vegetable oil
2 medium onions, chopped
1 cup light brown sugar
1 cup apple juice
1/4 cup apple cider vinegar
1 12-ounce bag fresh cranberries
1 orange
2 tablespoons fresh, grated ginger
3 medium pears, cored, peeled and cut into 1/2-inch pieces
1 cup chopped dried apricots or dried cherries

Heat vegetable oil in a wide pot over medium heat. Add onion and cook until translucent and beginning to brown, about 15 minutes. Add sugar, apple juice, vinegar and cranberries. Grate orange part of the orange peel and add to mixture, along with the juice from the orange. Stir to dissolve sugar. Add remaining ingredients and bring to a boil. Reduce heat and cook until mixture is thick, about 30 minutes. Refrigerate two weeks or freeze for longer storage. Makes about 6 cups.

MASHED POTATOES

There are only a few challenges to making perfect mashed potatoes: lumps, viscosity and, of course, the time to do it.

Lumps can be avoided with several tools. My mother used a ricer. A ricer looks like a giant garlic press, with a metal plunger that presses potatoes through a metal basket with holes in it. You can find ricers at some cookware shops and hardware stores.

Or mash potatoes with a hand-held masher, then whip until fluffy with a whisk or electric beaters. Very tender potatoes can be whipped lump-free with an electric mixer, but are fairly compact (an easy trade-off for effort and time involved).

Add liquid and butter after the potatoes are mashed (they'll get lumps if you do it before).

Some tips for making mashed potatoes:

• To hasten the process, cook peeled potato chunks in a wide pan that holds the potatoes in a shallow layer. Add enough water to keep them moist and cook them, then whip right in the pan with an electric mixer. Season with salt, pepper, butter and cream or milk, if desired.

• Potatoes can be made fat-free by using the broth you cooked them in, chicken broth or skim milk as your whipping liquid.

• Leftovers can be used to make rolls or potato-cheese soup (thin with milk or chicken broth, add sautéed onions and grated sharp cheese).

• It takes about 3 pounds of potatoes to make 6 cups mashed. The potatoes that come in the 5- and 10-pound net bags at the supermarket usually weigh between 5 and 7 ounces each. It's up to you how much makes a serving—health professionals say 1/2 cup of mashed potatoes is a serving, but in our house grown-ups eat more.

The amount of liquid required to make fluffy mashed potatoes varies with the potato; in these classic mashed potatoes we give you approximate measurements.

11 medium potatoes
2 teaspoons salt
4 tablespoons butter
3/4 cup milk, skim milk or potato-cooking liquid
Freshly ground pepper, to taste

Peel potatoes and cut them into 6 chunks each. Boil them in water to cover, adding 1 teaspoon of salt. When they are tender (15 minutes or so), drain, saving liquid if desired.

Mash the potatoes by desired method, then add up to another teaspoon of salt, 4 tablespoons butter, 3/4 cup milk or potato-cooking liquid and pepper to taste. Serve hot. Serves 8.

SWEET POTATO CASSEROLE

For some, sweet potato casserole makes the Thanksgiving meal. We offer a less-sweet version below.

4 pounds sweet potatoes
1 teaspoon salt
1 lemon
3/4 cup brown sugar
2 eggs, beaten
1/2 teaspoon nutmeg
1/2 cup whole milk
1/2 cup chopped pecans
1/2 cup butter, melted
Miniature marshmallows

Peel sweet potatoes and cut them about 1/2-inch thick. Place in a saucepan, cover with water, and add salt. Bring to a boil, reduce heat and cover until tender, about 15 minutes. Drain, then mash the potatoes with a hand masher and use a mixer to whip them (or mash them in the way you prefer).

Heat oven to 350 degrees. Grate the lemon rind (yellow part only), into a large bowl. Cut the lemon in half and squeeze the lemon juice into the bowl. Add sugar, eggs, nutmeg, milk, pecans, and butter. Add sweet potatoes and stir to combine. Transfer sweet potatoes to a 9- by 13-inch (or similar) casserole. Bake for 25 minutes. Top with marshmallows and bake 5 to 10 more minutes, or until marshmallows are golden brown.

SESAME SWEET POTATOES

If you want to make not-too-sweet potatoes, try this recipe. It was dubbed ''the best way I've ever eaten sweet potatoes'' by one skeptic. It draws on some Asian flavors to complement the sweetness of the potatoes. If you've never seasoned sweet potatoes with ginger, you're missing something. Use a teaspoon of dried ginger if you don't have fresh.

Sweet potatoes benefit from long, slow roasting. Their texture becomes creamy and the flesh becomes sweeter.

5 large sweet potatoes, about 2 1/2 pounds

1/4 cup vegetable oil

2 teaspoons sesame seeds

Salt and (freshly ground) pepper

1 tablespoon finely chopped or grated fresh ginger

2 tablespoons honey

1 cup orange juice

1 tablespoon soy sauce

Heat oven to 400 degrees. Cut off the pointy tips of the sweet potatoes and discard. Peel sweet potatoes; cut them into 1-inch chunks. Put them in a wide casserole, such as a 9- by 13-inch baking pan. Drizzle with vegetable oil and stir the potatoes, turning to coat them with oil. Sprinkle with sesame seeds, salt and pepper. Combine ginger, honey, orange juice and soy sauce; stir to dissolve honey and pour over potatoes. Cover with a lid or foil and bake for 30 minutes. Uncover the potatoes, stir and bake 30 minutes more, stirring every 10 minutes. Serves 10.

PUMPKIN PIE

For this and future crust making success, follow the advice of a blue-ribbon winner from the Kentucky State Fair: store your vegetable shortening in the freezer. It remains easy to dip and measure, but you'll extend its shelf life and ensure that it's cold for pie crust. Or substitute a store-bought crust, if you prefer.

Crust:
1 cup all-purpose flour
1/2 teaspoon salt
1/3 cup chilled shortening
1 tablespoon cold butter
2 to 3 tablespoons water

Filling:
3 eggs
1 15-ounce can pumpkin (about 1 2/3 cups purée)
3/4 cup light brown sugar
1/2 teaspoon salt
1 teaspoon ginger
1/2 teaspoon ground cloves
1/2 teaspoon cinnamon
12 ounces evaporated milk
Heavy (whipping) cream, optional

To make the crust: Combine the flour and salt in a medium-size bowl. Add half the shortening and use a pastry blender or two knives to cut it into the flour until it resembles coarse meal. Add remaining shortening and the butter and cut until the largest pieces are the size of small peas.

Add water and stir to combine. You should be able to gather the dough in a ball. If you need to add a little more water, do so, a couple of teaspoons should do it. Use a rolling pin and roll the dough on a lightly-floured surface or on a piece of plastic wrap to about 10 1/2-inches in diameter, or large enough to fill your pie pan. Press gently into pan and trim edges. Chill or freeze until needed.

Heat oven to 400 degrees. Spray the dull side of aluminum foil with cooking spray. Press into cold pie shell and fill with beans, pie weights or nuts and bolts (nothing sharp) from the your work bench. Bake the pie crust for 20 minutes. Remove foil and weights (you can use the beans later for cooking). Reduce oven heat to 350, put the crust in the oven and bake 5 more minutes. Remove crust.

To make the filling: Place the eggs in a bowl and beat lightly. Add pumpkin and stir to blend. Add sugar and spices and stir again. Stir in milk. Pour into pie crust and bake 40 minutes, or until only the center jiggles ever so slightly when you shake the pie gently. Cool, then refrigerate. Serve with sweetened or unsweetened whipped cream.

CHOCOLATE CREAM PIE

It's a family tradition at Thanksgiving. I usually whip cream to use as the topping. The cream isn't as sweet as the meringue and makes a refreshing counterpoint to the chocolate. But if you like meringue you'll love this recipe. It doesn't weep, and it takes days in the refrigerator to show beads on the top. It's as foolproof as I've found.

Crust:
1 cup all-purpose flour
1/2 teaspoon salt
1/3 cup chilled shortening
1 tablespoon cold butter
2 to 3 tablespoons water

Meringue:
1 tablespoon cornstarch
1/2 cup sugar
1/2 cup water
3 egg whites
Dash of salt

Filling:
1/3 cup flour
1 cup sugar
1/4 teaspoon salt
2 cups milk
3 egg yolks
4 ounces unsweetened chocolate
4 tablespoons butter
1/2 teaspoon vanilla
1 9-inch baked pastry shell

To make the crust: Combine the flour and salt in a medium-size bowl. Add half the shortening and use a pastry blender or two knives to cut it into the flour until it resembles coarse meal. Add remaining shortening and the butter and cut until the largest pieces are the size of small peas. Add water and stir to combine. You should be able to gather the dough in a ball. If you need to add a little more water, do so, a couple of teaspoons should do it. Use a rolling pin and roll the dough on a lightly-floured surface or on a piece of plastic wrap to about 10 1/2-inches in diameter, or large enough to fill your pie pan. Press gently into pan and trim edges. Chill or freeze until needed.

Heat oven to 400 degrees. Spray the dull side of aluminum foil with cooking spray. Press into cold pie shell and fill with beans, pie weights or nuts and bolts (nothing sharp) from the your work bench. Bake the pie crust for 20 minutes. Remove foil and weights (you can use the beans later for cooking). Reduce oven heat to 350, put the crust in the oven and bake until light brown, 20 to 30 minutes. Remove crust.

To make the filling: In a heavy saucepan, combine flour, sugar and salt. Stir to break up the flour. Stir in milk. Cook over medium-low heat, stirring frequently, until the mixture comes to a slow boil and thickens considerably. Meanwhile, beat the egg yolks to break them up in a small bowl. When the milk mixture has thickened, add about 1/2 cup to the egg yolks and stir quickly to blend. Stir the egg yolks into the milk mixture and cook a minute or so, stirring. Remove from heat, add chocolate and butter and stir frequently until they melt and blend into the custard. Mix in vanilla and pour into baked pie shell.

To make meringue: Combine cornstarch, 2 tablespoons sugar and water in a small saucepan and cook over low heat until the mixture boils and is translucent. Remove from heat. In a bowl, beat egg whites until soft peaks form, then add the cornstarch mixture little by little, beating it in as you do. Add salt and remaining sugar and beat until fluffy. Spread on pie and bake at 350 degrees until meringue has brown peaks, 20 minutes or so. Serves 6 to 8.

Turkey Fried Rice

TURKEY LEFTOVERS

Like taxes, turkey leftovers are as predictable as they are unavoidable.

For every Thanksgiving table there is a turkey carcass being readied for everything from refrigerators to landfills.

A little knowledge will not only prevent them from becoming garbage, it can turn a carcass into a great dinner. Knowing how to store leftovers will keep the meat and bones in good condition until you use them. Just as important is knowing how good the leftovers can taste—to my mind, even better than the original bird.

Turkey leftovers should be dealt with promptly after dinner is served. The turkey should not be out of the oven more than two hours before it is wrapped and refrigerated or frozen. If you have stuffed the bird (and we recommend that you don't), scrape all of the dressing from the cavity and refrigerate or freeze it separately. It is safe to freeze this dressing, even if it has an egg in it, but follow the 2-hour rule.

Food experts will tell you that leftovers should be used within three days. Thrifty cooks will tell you that leftovers last longer. Whomever you believe, be practical. If you're not going to eat all of the leftover turkey in the next few days, freeze the extra to use later. At the very least, cover the turkey well with foil (trapped air is the enemy of good frozen food) and stick it in the freezer.

To freeze your turkey for future use: Remove all the meat you can from the bones. Slice off the breast meat, slice up the thigh meat and pull off any bits you think will be useful for salads or casseroles. Wrap or package these in useful portions—a pound of slices for future Hot Browns, a container of pieces for turkey salad.

Many cooks will find that though they have no time to make homemade soup on the average day, Thanksgiving weekend finds them at home with just the time they need to make turkey soup and sandwiches.

You don't need leftover turkey. All of these recipes can be made with canned chicken broth and cut up chicken breast. Or if you'd like to make turkey salad for a summer lunch, roast a turkey breast (or cook it in the slow cooker to keep the kitchen cooler). Likewise, if you'd like to make a soup, choose a bony part—turkey wing or drumstick—and make the broth with that.

TURKEY BROTH

If the directions on the following soup look complicated, think of it this way: broth is nothing more than bones and bits of meat simmered in water for a long time. Bones will yield a gelatin of sorts that firms the broth when it is chilled. The more concentrated the broth, the more flavorful the soup will be (and the firmer your chilled broth may be). If you combine a turkey carcass in a stockpot with 4 gallons of water, you will get a weaker broth than if you put it in a 5-quart Dutch oven with 2 or 3 quarts of water. We tend to start with lots of water and let it boil down (reduce) to concentrate the flavor. But you can't really go wrong.

To make broth:

Separate the turkey pieces at all the joints, then crack the body into two or three pieces. Place these bones (they will still have meat attached) in your largest pot and cover the turkey pieces with water. (This may require two pots, depending on the size of your pots and the size of your turkey.) Bring the water to a boil, reduce heat to low and simmer, uncovered, an hour or two. Remove the bones to a plate and allow them to cool.

You can cool the broth at this point and freeze it or use it for soup. Or continue to let it simmer, which will evaporate the water and concentrate the flavors. The final broth will take up less room in your freezer.

When the bones are cool enough to handle, remove all the meat from them that you can or care to salvage. Discard fat, skin and bone. Freeze the extras to use later, or use them to make this flavorful soup.

TURKEY SOUP

This soup is the recipe I devised after Thanksgiving one year. People who focus on health will notice the nutritious qualities of the soup, the cancer-fighting ability of cabbage, carrot and turnip, the artery-friendliness of the fibers in beans and barley, the leanness of leftover turkey, the blood-thinning capabilities of onion.

But this is just good food, and a clever way to get the kids to eat turnips. None of the vegetables is absolutely essential. Don't make a special trip to the store for a carrot, for instance. Same with the beans—use white or red beans if you prefer, or if they're handy.

4 tablespoons turkey fat, butter or vegetable oil
1 onion
1 carrot
1 rib celery
1 turnip
1/2 small white cabbage
1 teaspoon dried thyme
1 bay leaf
3 quarts turkey broth
1/3 cup barley or rice
2 cups (or so) cooked garbanzo beans (also called chickpeas)
2 cups (or so) leftover turkey (especially good with dark meat)
2 teaspoons salt
1 teaspoon (freshly ground) pepper

Heat turkey fat, butter or oil in the bottom of a 4 1/2- quart pot or Dutch oven. Peel and dice onion. Add it to fat and cook over medium heat as

(continued)

you trim, peel and chop carrot and add to pot. Chop celery; add to pot and stir occasionally as the vegetables cook. Trim and mince turnip; add to pot.

Remove core from cabbage and sliver cabbage with a sharp knife. Add to pot. Cook the vegetables until they are tender. Add thyme, bay leaf and 3 quarts turkey broth (or whatever fits). Bring to a boil. Add barley or rice and cook 30 minutes. Add beans, turkey, salt and pepper. Heat through. Taste for seasoning and add salt and pepper as needed. When barley (or rice) is tender and soup is hot, serve or store for later use. Makes about a gallon of soup. It freezes well.

TURKEY STOCK

You don't have to bolster turkey broth with vegetables. You can simply simmer bones and water and create a good base for soup. Or add some seasoning as we have here. In either case, strain and freeze for future use, or freeze within 3 days.

1 turkey carcass
1 onion
1 carrot
1 rib celery

Break up the turkey carcass. Use all the bones you have collected—wings, thigh and drumstick too. Place in your largest pot (ideally one that holds at least 2 gallons). Add 6 quarts of water, or more, to cover the carcass. Peel onion, quarter, and add to pot. Trim carrot and celery and cut each into 4 pieces; add to pot. Cover the pot with a lid, bring to a boil; uncover and simmer on lowest heat for 3 hours or so. Strain broth.

Allow the broth to continue to simmer (it's reducing and concentrating flavors). When the bones are cool enough to handle, remove any edible meat and place in a small bowl for use later in soups, casseroles, etc. Discard bone, skin and cartilage. You want to reduce the turkey broth to about 3 quarts by letting the liquid evaporate as the soup simmers uncovered. When the broth is reduced, strain again.

Chill the broth. Remove any fat that hardens on top. The cooled broth may be separated into smaller containers for freezing. If it turns to jelly when it's cool, that's a good thing. Makes 3 quarts.

QUICK TURKEY AND POTATO SOUP

This delicious soup can be made with canned chicken broth and chicken meat, if you like. Follow the recipe, adding the chicken chunks at the end when the turkey is called for, and simmer about 10 minutes, stirring occasionally, to allow the chicken to cook through. Ten minutes should be plenty of time to cook the chicken without making it dry.

> 4 slices bacon, diced
> 1 medium onion, diced
> 2 ribs celery, trimmed of tough ends and diced
> 3 medium potatoes, peeled and chopped about 1/2-inch square
> 1 quart turkey broth (or substitute 2 15- or 16-ounce cans chicken broth)
> 1-pound bag frozen corn (about 3 cups)
> 2 cups diced, cooked turkey (or chicken)
> Salt and (freshly ground) pepper, to taste

Put the bacon in a large, heavy saucepan and place over medium heat. As the bacon cooks, dice onion and celery. When bacon is fairly crisp, remove it to a paper towel to drain. Discard all but 2 tablespoons of the fat in the pan (or add vegetable oil to make 2 tablespoons).

Add the onion and celery to the pan and cook over medium heat. As they cook, peel and dice the potatoes. When the celery and onion have softened, increase the heat to high, add potatoes and turkey broth. Bring to a boil, reduce heat to simmer and cook about 30 minutes.

Meanwhile, combine 2 cups of corn and 1 cup of water in a blender and blend a little but so that some small chunks of corn remain. Add to pot with remaining corn. When the potatoes are tender, add the turkey and cook to heat through. Season with salt and pepper to taste. Crumble bacon on top. Serves 6.

To make the soup richer: Add a cup of cream.

THAI TURKEY SOUP

I love Thai food, so I'm happy that many easy-to-use Thai ingredients are available in the supermarket. This soup refreshingly changes the personality of turkey leftovers, from down-home to exotic, and it requires only a can of coconut milk and a spoon full of Thai curry paste from a jar. Lemon grass is great, but you can omit it.

1 1/2 quarts (6 cups) turkey broth (or substitute reduced-sodium chicken broth)
10 thin slices fresh ginger, about the size of a quarter
1 or 2 stems lemon grass, optional
1 13- or 14-ounce can unsweetened coconut milk
1 or 2 tablespoons green or red curry paste
1 tablespoon brown sugar
2 tablespoons fish sauce or soy sauce
2 cups cut up or shredded cooked turkey
1 cup (lightly packed) fresh baby spinach
1 serrano chili, sliced into thin rounds (optional, the curry paste will be hot)
Fresh cilantro, chopped

Combine turkey broth with 1 cup of water and ginger in a saucepan. Bring to a boil over high heat, then reduce to simmer.

Cut the tough tops (at least 8 or 10 inches) off the lemongrass, and trim the root. Cut the remaining piece into 2-inch lengths. With the back of a heavy knife or another blunt object, bruise the leaves. Add them to the broth.

Shake well the can of coconut milk. Pour about 1/2 of it into a large pot set over high heat. Add curry paste. Stir to work out the lumps. Add sugar, fish sauce and turkey. Pour the turkey broth through a strainer into the coconut milk. Add remaining milk to the pot, along with spinach. Cook until spinach is wilted. Serve topped with chili slices (if desired) and cilantro. Serves 4.

TURKEY TORTILLA SOUP

Another way to turn holiday leftovers into non-holiday tasting soup. Thicken the soup with lots of chips to make it more substantial.

    1 medium onion
    3 to 4 large cloves garlic, about 2 teaspoons, minced
    2 tablespoons oil
    1 1/2 quarts (6 cups) turkey broth (or substitute reduced-sodium chicken broth)
    2 cups (or so) cut up or shredded turkey or chicken
    2 cups tomato salsa (heat level is your choice)
    Salt and (freshly ground) pepper to taste
    3 ounces (or so) tortilla chips (low-fat work well)
    Optional garnishes: grated Muenster cheese, minced cilantro, sour cream, hot sauce, minced onion, minced jalapeno pepper, etc.

Dice onion. Mince garlic. Heat oil in Dutch oven or large pot over medium-high heat. Add onion and cook, stirring occasionally, about 5 minutes. Add garlic. Cook a minute or so. Add turkey broth, turkey, salsa and 1 cup water. Bring to a boil, reduce heat and simmer 8 to 10 minutes. Taste for seasoning, adding salt and pepper if desired. Place a handful of tortilla chips into each of 4 serving bowls. Ladle soup into bowl. Garnish with toppings as desired. Serves 4.

TURKEY MELT

Now we all know that turkey sandwiches made with cranberry sauce and mayonnaise are the very essence of turkey leftovers, but this sandwich is also good.

2 slices bacon
2 English muffin halves
2 teaspoons butter or mayonnaise
2 thin slices turkey
About 1/3 cup grated sharp cheddar cheese

Cut bacon in half to make 4 short pieces. Put in a small skillet and cook over medium heat until not quite crisp.

Meanwhile, put oven rack about 4 inches from broiler unit. Heat broiler. Spread each cut side of English muffin with butter or mayonnaise. Toast lightly. Place a slice of turkey on the split side of each muffin. Pat a layer of cheddar cheese on top. Top each half with 2 slices bacon. Put under broiler until cheese melts. Serves 1 as a sandwich, 2 as a side dish to soup or salad.

TURKEY TOSTADA

Amounts are approximate – use your judgment.

1 large (8-or 9-inch) flour tortilla or 2 corn tortillas
3 tablespoons salsa
1/3 cup grated Colby or Muenster cheese
1/4 cup shredded or diced turkey
Red or green salsa or hot sauce

Heat oven to 400 degrees. Put a large flour tortilla on a pizza pan or other flat pan and toast 3 or 4 minutes. Spread with salsa and sprinkle with cheese. Top with turkey, diced small. Heat until cheese is bubbly and melted. Serve with spicy salsa or sauce. Serves 1.

TURKEY SALAD

3 cups shredded or diced turkey (preferably a combination of dark and white meat)
1 cup finely diced celery
1/2 cup mayonnaise, approximately
1 teaspoon salt
1/2 teaspoon cayenne pepper

Combine ingredients. Serves 4. Add more mayonnaise if you like.

Curried Turkey Salad:
Add 1 teaspoon curry powder and 1 firm, crisp apple, diced small.

TURKEY FRIED RICE

Fried rice is a great way to use up leftovers of any kind—a pork chop, some breakfast sausage, just about anything. The trick: make sure the rice is cold before you make the fried rice.

Feel free to use another vegetable instead of broccoli in the recipe below: cabbage, carrots, snow peas, mushrooms; anything works, but they cook at different rates.

2 cups long-grain white rice
1 teaspoon salt
3 tablespoons soy sauce
1 teaspoon sugar
2 teaspoons vinegar
1 teaspoon sesame oil
1/2 teaspoon hot red pepper flakes, or hot seasoning, optional
3 tablespoons turkey fat or vegetable oil
1 medium onion, cut into 1/2-inch pieces, approximately
1 teaspoon fresh, minced ginger
2 to 3 cloves fresh garlic, minced, about 1 1/2 teaspoons
2 cups broccoli florets, cut small
2 to 3 cups cubed or shredded cooked turkey (or chicken)

Put 4 cups of water on to boil with 1 teaspoon salt. When it boils, add rice, cover, reduce heat and simmer about 18 minutes. Cool, then chill in refrigerator until cold and hard.

Mix soy sauce, sugar, vinegar, sesame oil, and red pepper flakes and stir to dissolve sugar. Set aside.

(continued)

Heat skillet or wok over high heat for 1 minute. Add fat to wok and put over high heat. Add onion and cook 2 minutes without stirring – you want pieces to brown a little, but don't let them burn. Stir them if it appears they might. Cook the onion 5 minutes more, stirring occasionally, so that edges get brown and some threaten to char. Add ginger and garlic and cook a minute, stirring. Add broccoli and 2 tablespoons of water and cook, stirring, about 3 minutes. Crumble rice into the wok, add turkey, and soy sauce mixture. Stir to heat through. Serves 4 to 6.

With egg: To make fried rice with bits of egg, beat 2 eggs briefly. Fry them in a little oil first until they are firm. Remove and proceed with onions.

HOT BROWN CASSEROLE

Louisville natives know Hot Browns as the sandwich made famous by the Brown Hotel.

2 cups toasted bread cubes, from bakery-style bread
2 cups diced, cooked turkey breast

Sauce:
1/2 cup butter
2/3 cup flour
1 teaspoon salt
1 teaspoon (freshly ground) pepper
4 cups milk, low-fat will work
3 cups shredded sharp cheddar cheese

Topping:
1/2 cup shredded Parmesan cheese
4 slices bacon, cooked then crumbled
1 cup diced tomatoes or cut-up cherry tomatoes

Heat oven to 350 degrees. Place bread cubes in the bottom of a 2-quart casserole. Top with diced turkey. Set aside.

To make the sauce: Melt butter in a medium sized pan. Add flour, salt and pepper and stir to blend. Slowly whisk in milk. The mixture will be thick and hard to stir at first; just stir the milk in little by little until it loosens up, then add the rest of the milk all at once. Continue to cook and stir until mixture bubbles. Remove from heat and add cheddar cheese. Stir until melted and the mixture is smooth. Pour sauce over bread and turkey. Sprinkle with Parmesan cheese, then with bacon and tomato bits. Bake 20 to 25 minutes, or until the casserole is hot and bubbly. Serves 6.

Grating orange rind

NEIGHBOR PARTY

Having the neighbors over is the most relaxed kind of party. I don't have to clean that well—they see the house all the time, they know what it looks like. And they love catching up on what we've all been doing during the cold weather when we don't see each other outside. Everyone feels at home.

So I'm calling this a neighbor party, but you might want to call it a tree-trimming party, or change the drinks to iced tea and lemonade and call it a graduation party. It's a party that accommodates a sizable crowd with an informal meal, letting people nosh and talk, and allows you to enjoy the party, too.

The neighbors surrounding me have children the same ages as mine, so they were invited to the first party. Each year I try to include another set of neighbors I didn't know so well. Now we give equinox parties so the larger crowd can spill onto the deck.

Mulled Cider
Egg Nog
Horseradish Cheese Spread
Spice-Rubbed Beef Roast on Store-Bought Buns
Sweet and Sour Green Beans
Orange Ginger Walnut Cake

MULLED CIDER

2 cinnamon sticks
4 cups apple juice or cider
1/2 cup honey
3 oranges, thinly sliced
3 lemons, thinly sliced
1/4 teaspoon ground cloves
1/4 teaspoon grated nutmeg
1/4 teaspoon ground allspice
5 tea bags

Combine cinnamon sticks with 5 cups water in a large enameled or stainless-steel pot. Bring to a boil over high heat. Reduce heat to simmer and add remaining ingredients except tea bags. Simmer 10 minutes. Remove from heat, add tea and allow the mixture to steep 5 minutes. Remove and discard tea bags.

To serve on a buffet, strain the hot mixture into a slow cooker set on low (you can float fresh citrus slices on the top, if desired). Put a ladle in the slow cooker so guests may serve themselves. Or strain into individual heated cups and garnish with cinnamon sticks. Serve with sides of bourbon and rum, if you like, for those who'd like to make a hot toddy.

Serves 8 to 10.

EGG NOG

Old recipes for egg nog called for separating eggs, beating the raw egg yolks with sugar, then adding milk and bourbon, and folding in stiffly beaten egg whites.

Cooked egg nog has replaced raw egg nog at our holiday parties. Though eggs that are contaminated with food-poisoning bacteria are exceedingly rare, raw-egg egg nog is not something you want to risk serving to guests and relatives. Besides, this tastes much richer and creamier.

6 eggs
1/3 cup sugar
Pinch salt
1 quart milk, divided
1 teaspoon vanilla
1 cup heavy (whipping) cream
Bourbon and rum

In large non-aluminum saucepan, beat together eggs, sugar and salt. Heat 2 cups of milk to boiling and, stirring constantly, add it in a slow stream to the eggs. Put the pan on low heat and stir constantly until the mixture is thick enough to coat a metal spoon with a thin film and reaches at least 160 degrees. Remove from heat, stir in 2 cups of cold milk and vanilla. Cover and chill completely. Just before serving, beat the heavy cream until fluffy mounds form. Fold into cold egg nog (some little pillows of cream can remain). Pour into bowl or pitcher. Serve bourbon and rum to the side for those who like to spike their nog, and a whole nutmeg with grater if you have them. Grating nutmeg on the top is a festive flourish. Serves 8.

(continued)

To prepare in a microwave: In 2-quart liquid measure or bowl, beat together eggs, sugar, and salt until thoroughly blended. Set aside. In 1-quart liquid measure or bowl, heat 2 cups of the milk on full power until bubbles form at edges, about 5 to 6 minutes. Stir into egg mixture. Cook on 50 percent power until mixture is thick enough to coat a metal spoon with a thin film and reaches at least 160 degrees, about 5 to 6 minutes, stirring and checking often. Stir in remaining 2 cups milk and vanilla. Continue as above.

HORSERADISH CHEESE SPREAD

This spicy cheese spread is easy to make and tastes great on rye crisp crackers or melbas.

3 cups (12 ounces) grated extra sharp cheddar cheese
8 ounces sour cream
4 tablespoons horseradish
2 tablespoons Worcestershire sauce
1 tablespoon Dijon mustard (or other spicy mustard)

Combine and mix or process until fairly smooth. Makes about 3 cups. Serve with crackers or thin slices of French bread.

SPICE-RUBBED BALTIMORE-STYLE BEEF ROAST

Are you one of those weirdos who will grill any time of year? You're not so rare any more. Now that gas-grill owners have surpassed the number of people buying charcoal grills, more people can grill without building a fire. People will love this beef if you prepare it on the grill, but it's also great from the oven.

Top round roast presents a lot of challenges. It is very lean and very tough, so it must be cooked no more than medium to serve as a roast. If you cook it to well done, you'll have the proverbial shoe leather on your hands. The thinner you can slice this roast, the better.

1 tablespoon seasoned salt
1 tablespoon paprika
1 teaspoon oregano
1/2 teaspoon cayenne pepper
1/2 teaspoon (freshly ground) black pepper
2 tablespoons minced fresh garlic
3 to 5 pounds top round roast

Heat oven to 500 degrees. Combine salt, paprika, oregano, cayenne and black pepper. Rub garlic over surface of roast. Sprinkle the roast all over with spice mixture to coat it as evenly as you can. Put in the oven, close the door, reduce heat to 400 and cook 40 minutes or until the roast is about 130 degrees internally, or cook to desired doneness. Let the roast stand 20 minutes before cutting it in ultra-thin slices. Serve on large buns for dinner, or small buns for a cocktail-buffet table. A 3-pound roast makes 48 3-inch sandwiches. (To cook on the grill, cook at 450 degrees to get it dark on the outside and keep it rare on the inside.) Note: You can rub on the spices and refrigerate the meat for several days before cooking. You can roast it ahead of time to serve the meat cold, or reheat it gently in a shallow roasting pan, covered.

SWEET AND SOUR GREEN BEANS

3 pounds green beans
1/2 pound bacon
1/2 cup vinegar, any will do
1 1/2 teaspoons salt
4 tablespoons sugar
1/2 teaspoon crushed red pepper flakes
1 cup (or so) diced red onion

Trim and wash the green beans (or use frozen). Break into 2-inch lengths.

Cut bacon in half to create short lengths. Place in a deep, wide pan that will hold all the beans and cook until crisp, in batches if you have to. Place on absorbent toweling.

Combine vinegar, salt, sugar and red pepper in a bowl and stir to start dissolving sugar.

Heat the pan over high heat. When the bacon fat is quite hot, add the red onion and stir about 1 minute. Add the beans and cook, stirring occasionally, about 5 to 10 minutes. The beans should be crisp-tender, and some can be brown and wrinkled in places. The time depends on how wide your pan is and how many of the beans are exposed to the heat at the bottom of the pan.

When the beans are done, spoon onto a platter. Pour vinegar mixture into pan and remove any bits stuck to the bottom of the pan by scraping with a spoon. Pour over beans. Scatter bacon bits over the top. Serves 12.

ORANGE GINGER WALNUT CAKE

This cake has introduced many people to the virtues of fresh ginger. You can use the powder, but the fresh is fabulous.

1 cup butter
2 cups sugar
2 large eggs
2 tablespoons freshly grated ginger, or 2 teaspoons dried
2 tablespoons orange liqueur (such as Grand Marnier) or 1 tablespoon orange juice concentrate
1 tablespoon finely grated orange peel (orange part only)
 2 cups all-purpose flour
1 teaspoon baking powder
1/2 teaspoon salt
1/2 teaspoon ground cloves
8 ounces (1 scant cup) sour cream
1 teaspoon vanilla
1 1/2 cups coarsely chopped walnuts

Heat oven to 350 degrees. Butter and flour a 10-inch tube pan or bundt pan. In a large bowl, beat the butter until fluffy. Add the sugar, pouring it gradually as you beat. Add eggs, one at a time, beating and scraping the sides of the bowl after each addition. Add ginger, orange liqueur and orange peel and beat briefly. Combine flour, baking powder, salt, and cloves in a bowl or on a piece of wax paper. Add 3/4 cup of flour to the butter mixture and stir it in. Add half the container of sour cream and stir it in completely. Repeat steps, ending with flour, then stir in vanilla and walnuts. Spoon into prepared pan and bake 75 minutes, or until a toothpick inserted into the center comes out clean. Cool in pan 20 minutes, then turn out onto rack and cool completely. Serves 12 to 14.

Making crust for cheesecake

SOUP SUPPER

Soup suppers are great for any winter entertaining, from caroling parties to February doldrums get-togethers. We have a neighbor who entertains with soup suppers, laying out cheese plates and desserts and putting large stock pots on portable burners. Or you can fill your slow-cookers with soup, turning the heat to high and leaving the top off.

I love soups because they are, in general, good for you yet, once they are made, they are as fast to grab as something junky. Soups fill you up fast, yet make you feel you've eaten something real, and homemade soups are always delicious. Leftovers usually freeze well. And I love cooking them because you can't really mess them up. They just push all my buttons.

Though two of the following soups are made with chicken broth, you can make all of them vegetarian with vegetable broth, or you can make them heartier by adding meat to them.

If you are holding your soup supper in the middle of holiday season, you certainly don't need to set out chocolate cheesecake. A few Christmas cookies and candies will suffice. Unless, of course, chocolate cheesecake is really the meaning of life. Which it can be.

Very Best White Bread
Chile-Cheese Cornbread
Tomato Artichoke Soup
Curried Corn Bisque
Chunky Mushroom Barley Soup
Chocolate Cheesecake

VERY BEST WHITE BREAD

No doubt you have a very good bakery in town where you can buy excellent bread for your soup supper. But if you'd like to try your hand at making your own, this is one of my favorite recipes. There was a time when I made it every Saturday. It's an old-fashioned white bread, soft and aromatic.

1 cup milk
1 cup water
2 tablespoons butter plus more for brushing loaves
2 tablespoons sugar
2 teaspoons salt
1 package dry yeast (about 2 1/2 teaspoons)
6 1/2 cups all-purpose flour, approximately

Combine milk with water, butter, sugar and salt and put over medium heat, stirring occasionally, until the butter melts and the sugar dissolves. Set aside to cool. Put 1/4 cup water in a small cup and sprinkle yeast over it. Stir to dissolve the yeast and set aside.

Put 3 cups of flour in a large bowl. When the milk is lukewarm or cooler, stir it into the flour. Beat it well for 1 or 2 minutes. Stir in yeast. Add another cup of flour and stir it in. Keep adding flour until the mixture is too stiff to stir. Sprinkle a little flour on a clean counter and place dough on counter. Flatten the dough with the heel of your hand and sprinkle it with some of the remaining flour. Fold the dough over, turn it a quarter turn, flatten and fold again. Keep flattening and folding (and sprinkling on any extra flour) until the dough is smooth. Flatten and fold a full minute or more after the last flour has been used. The dough should pull away

from the counter nicely and be smooth and elastic, not sticky. Place in a lightly greased bowl, brush the top with melted butter, cover the bowl with plastic wrap and allow the mixture to rise until doubled in bulk, about 1 hour at room temperature (or overnight in the fridge).

Punch dough down, and divide it in half. Fold and flatten as you did before until dough reaches its original size. Set aside again to rise, about 1 1/2 hours. Divide the dough in half, shape into loaves and put them in greased 8 1/2- by 4 1/2-inch loaf pans. Let the dough rise again for about 45 to 60 minutes.

Heat the oven to 450 degrees. When it's hot, put the risen loaves in it and bake 10 minutes. Reduce heat to 350 and bake 30 minutes more. Remove from the oven and run a knife around the sides of the pan. Tip the bread out, brush all surfaces generously with melted butter, and put back on the oven rack (no pan) for 15 minutes. The top crust should be a rich brown. Place loaves on a rack to cool, and cool completely before slicing with a serrated knife. Makes 2 loaves, about 10 generous slices each.

CHILI-CHEESE CORNBREAD

This cornbread stays moist at room temperature, which makes it good for a buffet. It is not spicy. If you like spice, add a minced jalapeno or some hot pepper sauce. Add a teaspoon of chili powder if the idea appeals to you.

**3 tablespoons butter
1 egg
8 ounces (1 scant cup) sour cream
1 4-ounce can chopped green chilies
1 1/2 cups yellow cornmeal
1/2 cup all-purpose flour
1 teaspoon baking soda
1/2 teaspoon salt
1 cup grated sharp cheddar cheese**

Heat oven to 350 degrees. Put butter in an 8- by 8-inch square baking dish or 8-inch iron skillet and place in the oven to melt butter.

In a medium bowl, beat the egg. Stir in sour cream and chilies. Remove pan from oven and tip it to coat the sides of the pan, then pour excess butter into cream mixture. Add cornmeal, flour, soda, and salt and stir several times. Add cheese and stir to blend. Pour into pan and bake for 30 minutes, or until brown spots appear on top. Makes 8 or 9 pieces.

TOMATO-ARTICHOKE SOUP

In my years writing for the newspaper, tomato-artichoke soup has been one of my most-requested recipes. There are many different versions, this one is delicious and not too much work. Whole milk makes a luscious soup, but you can use reduced-fat milk if you prefer.

1/3 cup olive oil
1 medium onion, about 1 cup diced
1/2 cup all-purpose flour
2 cups chicken stock or water
3 cups whole milk
1 tablespoon basil
3/4 teaspoon oregano
1 teaspoon salt
1 teaspoon (freshly ground) black pepper
14 ounces canned (not marinated) artichoke hearts
28 ounces canned crushed tomatoes

Heat olive oil in a large pot. Add diced onion and cook over medium heat, stirring occasionally, until the onion is transparent, about 5 minutes. Add flour and stir to mix.

Slowly stir in chicken broth. The mixture will tighten up and be hard to stir, just add little splashes of the broth and keep stirring. As the mixture loosens you can add the chicken broth faster. Add milk, basil, oregano, salt and pepper and stir to blend. Bring to a boil, reduce heat, then simmer 10 minutes.

Drain artichoke hearts and cut into small pieces. Add to soup along with tomatoes. Heat through and serve. Serves 6. Doubles easily.

CURRIED CORN BISQUE

Make this easy soup in summer when fresh corn is available and serve with BLTs.

2 tablespoons vegetable oil
1 medium onion, chopped
1 tablespoon curry powder
1/2 teaspoon Tabasco
1/2 teaspoon salt
1/4 teaspoon (freshly ground) black pepper
3 10-ounce packages frozen corn (substitute 6 cups fresh)
4 cups chicken broth, water or combination
1/2 cup half and half (nonfat works)

Heat vegetable oil in a saucepan set over medium-high heat. Add chopped onions and, stirring occasionally, cook about 5 minutes or until onions are soft and translucent. Add curry powder, Tabasco, salt, and pepper and stir to coat onions. Add corn and chicken broth and bring to a boil. Remove from heat and pour some into blender. Blend in batches until not completely smooth, but a little creamier. Add half and half and heat through. Taste and add more salt and hot sauce if necessary. Makes about 8 cups. Doubles easily.

To make this soup with meat: omit the curry powder and add 1/2 pound of breakfast sausage to the onion as it's cooking. Drain any excess fat before continuing with the recipe.

CHUNKY MUSHROOM BARLEY SOUP

This broth is an excellent starting point for many vegetarian soups. If you have excess potato peels, add them.

If you have bones from a standing rib roast, or other piece of beef (or lamb), you can add it to the broth ingredients if you like.

Broth:
1 medium onion
2 carrots
1 rib celery
1 teaspoon thyme
1 head garlic, broken into cloves but not peeled

Soup:
1 ounce dried porcini or morels, optional
2 tablespoons olive or vegetable oil
1 medium onion, peeled and diced
1 turnip, peeled and minced
1 pound fresh mushrooms
1/4 cup fresh, minced parsley
1 teaspoon dried dill
1 tablespoon soy sauce (Kikkomen or imported Chinese soy sauce)
Salt and (freshly ground) pepper to taste
1/2 cup uncooked pearl barley

For the broth: Bring 8 cups of water (and bones, if using) to a boil over high heat. Meanwhile, peel and quarter onion. Add to pot. Wash, trim and cut carrots into quarters. Wash and cut celery into large chunks. Add

(continued)

to pot along with thyme and garlic (unpeeled but with excess papery skin removed). Bring to a boil. Reduce heat and simmer 1 hour. Drain, discarding solids. Set aside or cool and freeze.

For the soup: Soak dried mushrooms (if using) in 1/2 cup hot water. Set aside. Heat oil in a large soup pot. Add onion and cook over medium heat. Mince turnip and add it. Clean and mince mushrooms and add them as you do. Stir after each addition. Add parsley, dill, soy sauce, vegetable broth and a little salt and pepper. Bring to a boil, add barley. Mince dried mushrooms, strain their soaking liquid and add both to soup. Reduce heat to low and simmer 1 hour. Taste and add salt and pepper as needed. Makes about 2 quarts.

To make this soup with meat: Cut a pound of chuck roast in 3 or 4 pieces. Add it to the broth ingredients and simmer. When you strain the soup, add the meat pieces back to the pot and simmer the additional hour. Remove meat and shred it using your fingers or 2 forks. Add meat back to soup.

CHOCOLATE CHEESECAKE

The directions below describe how to bake this cake in a water bath, that is, putting the pan into a larger pan and surrounding it with hot water. This barrier of water ensures that the cake heats gently and remains creamy smooth, minimizing the risk of cracking. I have made this cake without a water bath, however, and it works.

Using coffee instead of rum in the recipe makes this a mocha cheesecake.

Crust:
1 1/2 cups gingersnap or graham cracker crumbs
1/4 cup butter, melted

Filling:
6 ounces semisweet chocolate
2 ounces unsweetened chocolate
1/4 cup rum or coffee
1 1/2 pounds cream cheese, softened
1 cup sugar
4 eggs
1 teaspoon almond extract

Topping:
1 cup powdered sugar
1 cup sour cream

Combine crumbs with butter and stir until blended. Press it into the bottom of a 9- or 10-inch springform pan.

(continued)

Chocolate Cheesecake

Heat oven to 350 degrees. Bring a small pot of water to a boil. Wrap the bottom and sides of the springform pan in a double layer of heavy duty aluminum foil, pressing the foil tightly into the joint and bottom of the pan to make sure that no water from the bath seeps into the cake. Set aside.

Melt chocolates together over low heat or in a microwave and stir to blend. Add rum and stir to blend. Set aside.

Beat cream cheese with an electric mixer until smooth and fluffy. Add sugar, 1/4 cup at a time, beating well and then scraping the sides of the pan before the next addition. Add eggs, 1 at a time, beating slowly after each addition and scraping the sides of the bowl until all are mixed in. Blend in almond extract and chocolate mixture. Pour into crust.

Set the pan in a larger pan and pour in boiling water to come halfway up the sides of the pan. Bake 55 minutes to 1 hour, or until cake is slightly wobbly in the middle. If it has lost its wobble, it is overcooked. Remove it from the oven and cool.

Beat together powdered sugar and sour cream. Spread on the top of the cheesecake and chill 1 1/2 hours or until set. Run a knife between cake and pan; remove ring from the cake and serve. Serves 14 to 16.

Biscotti

COOKIES FOR HOLIDAYS AND EVERY DAY

People tend to dismiss the difficulty of a certain job or chore by saying, "Well, it's not exactly brain surgery." What they mean is you don't have to have too much skill, or concentration, or an exacting personality for the job at hand.

To me, those people who make huge and various batches of cookies over the holidays are the brain surgeons of the food world with skill, concentration and an eye for detail. I admire them and could never be one; I have no patience and I am the opposite of exacting—a bar-cookie gal, myself—spread them out, cut them up.

Cookie baking is a reality of the holidays, however, even for me. And for those people who find it easiest to conform to the demands of the season I provide a few necessary and favorite recipes here. It's a selection that can provide gifts for relatives away from home, ornament-making opportunities, and some tried-and-true basics that can make you look like a cookie-baking veteran. And with cookies, unlike brain surgery, there's no bad outcome if the knife slips.

Sugar Cookies
Esther's Ginger Cookies
Lime Zingers
Thumbprints
Chocolate Chocolate Chip
Anise Almond Biscotti
Bourbon Balls
Chocolate Oatmeal Bars
Peppermint Brownies

SUGAR COOKIES

This is classic dough for rolling and cutting out. Plan ahead, it must be chilled before rolling. If you're decorating with silver dragees, colored sugars and other press-on decorations, do that before they go into the oven. If you're icing them, ice when the cookies are fully cooled.

1 1/2 cups powdered sugar
1 cup butter
1 egg
1 teaspoon vanilla
1/2 teaspoon almond extract, optional
1/2 teaspoon baking powder
Pinch of salt
2 1/2 cups all-purpose flour

Beat sugar and butter in a large bowl. Add egg, vanilla and almond extract, if using. Stir in baking powder, salt and flour until well-combined. Cover the bowl with plastic wrap and refrigerate 2 hours to overnight (or freeze for later use).

Heat oven to 375 degrees. Break off 1/4 of the dough and roll it to about 1/8 inch thick (keep remaining dough chilled until using). Use a biscuit cutter or cookie cutters to cut out shapes. Place on ungreased cookie sheet and bake 7 to 8 minutes or until the cookies are browning on the edges. Press together scraps and refrigerate those as you roll out pieces of remaining dough. Altering the thickness of the dough can alter cooking time, as can some shapes—keep an eye on them. Makes 5 dozen 2 1/2-inch cookies.

ESTHER'S GINGER COOKIES

My mother-in-law sends us a huge container of these old-fashioned spice cookies every December. I love them, and am glad to have her recipe. They are soft cookies.

3/4 cup shortening
1 cup sugar
1 egg
1/3 cup molasses
2 cups all-purpose flour
1 1/2 teaspoons baking soda
1/2 teaspoon salt
1 teaspoon ginger
1 teaspoon cinnamon
Extra sugar for rolling

Beat shortening and sugar until blended, then beat in egg and molasses. Add flour, baking soda, salt, ginger and cinnamon and beat slowly or blend with a spoon until mixed completely. Cover tightly and chill at least an hour. Form into 1 1/2-inch balls and roll in sugar to coat, placing them 2 inches apart on a cookie sheet as you do. Bake 10 to 12 minutes.

LIME ZINGERS

Leave out the lime and add nuts and you'll have a basic Russian teacake cookie. The lime adds an unexpected surprise to a holiday cookie platter. Lime zest is the green part of the lime peel. To get the finest pieces, remove the zest with the rasp side of a box grater or with a micro-plane grater.

These cookies are fragile, melt in your mouth and may be the best of this selection.

> 1 cup butter
> 1/2 cup powdered sugar
> 1 3/4 cup all-purpose flour
> 1/4 cup cornstarch
> Grated zest of 1 lime
> 1/2 teaspoon vanilla
> Powdered sugar

Heat oven to 350 degrees Combine butter and sugar in a large bowl and beat until light and fluffy. Stir in flour, cornstarch, lime zest and vanilla. Blend well. Roll into 1-inch balls or drop by heaping teaspoons onto ungreased cookie sheet. Bake 10 minutes, or until edges are barely brown. Remove from cookie sheet and cool completely. Dust heavily with powdered sugar. Makes about 2 dozen.

THUMBPRINTS

Not too sweet and totally traditional. Chop the nuts very fine.

1/2 cup butter, softened
1/2 cup brown sugar
2 eggs, separated
1/8 teaspoon salt
1 teaspoon vanilla
2 cups all-purpose flour
1 1/2 cups finely chopped pecans, walnuts or almonds
Fruit preserves or chocolate frosting

Heat oven to 350 degrees.

In a large mixing bowl, combine butter, brown sugar, egg yolks, salt and vanilla. Beat until creamy. Add the flour and beat until completely mixed.

Beat egg whites in a saucer until foamy. Spread nuts on a plate. Form dough into 1-inch balls. Dip each ball into egg white, then roll in nuts to coat. Place 1 inch apart on ungreased cookie sheet and make a depression in the center of each with your thumb or the back of a teaspoon (they'll crack in a spot or two with the pressure—that's traditional). Bake 10 minutes. Remove cookies from oven and fill centers with jam or chocolate frosting. Makes about 3 dozen cookies.

CHOCOLATE CHOCOLATE CHIP COOKIES

These are very fragile cookies that are totally addictive.

1 cup sugar
3/4 cup brown sugar
3/4 cup butter
1/2 cup vegetable shortening
2 eggs
1 teaspoon vanilla
2 3/4 cups all-purpose flour
1/2 cup cocoa
1 teaspoon baking soda
1/4 teaspoon salt
1 1/2 cup chocolate morsels (milk, mint or semi-sweet)
1 cup chopped walnuts or pecans, optional

Heat oven to 350 degrees

Combine sugars, butter, shortening, eggs and vanilla and beat until creamy. Add flour, cocoa, soda, and salt and stir to mix well. Stir in morsels and nuts if using.

Drop by rounded tablespoons about 2 inches apart on an ungreased cookie sheet. Bake 10 to 12 minutes or until set. Cool slightly and remove from cookie sheet. Makes 4 to 5 dozen.

ANISE ALMOND BISCOTTI

These cookies are very crisp but not the super-hard style you sometimes find. You can bite through them easily.

Though anise is typical flavoring for these Italian cookies, not everyone loves its licorice flavor (I don't like licorice candy but I do love anise biscotti). If you'd like to make biscotti but not this type, omit the anise and add 2/3 cup dried cranberries to the dough when you stir in the cooled nuts.

Zest is the colored part of the citrus peel. Remove it with the rasp side of a grater or a micro-plane grater.

1 1/2 cups almonds
2 cups all-purpose flour
1 teaspoon baking powder
1/4 teaspoon salt
3/4 cup sugar
1 teaspoon anise seed
2 eggs
1/4 cup vegetable oil
2 teaspoons grated orange zest or 1 teaspoon grated lemon zest,
    optional
1 1/2 teaspoons vanilla

Heat oven to 350 degrees. Spread the almonds in an ungreased pan and put them in the oven (or on high power in the microwave) to toast, about 15 minutes or until they are light brown inside and aromatic. Chop them coarsely. Let them cool completely.

(continued)

Combine flour, baking powder, and salt in a bowl or on waxed paper. In a large bowl, beat sugar, anise and eggs until they are very light, a minute or so. Add vegetable oil, orange peel if using and vanilla. Beat to blend. Gradually add flour mixture and keep beating until all is incorporated. Stir in cooled nuts.

Turn dough onto lightly floured surface. Sprinkle with a teaspoon or two of flour and knead flour into dough. Shape into two logs that are about 8 to 10 inches long and 2 inches wide—the cookies do spread as they bake. Place 3 inches apart on a baking sheet. They should be slightly mounded in the middle, lower on the sides. Cook 25 minutes, or until light brown. Let the cookies cool about 20 minutes.

Cut the logs crosswise into 1/2-inch slices. Place slices cut side down on a cookie sheet. Bake 15 minutes, gently flipping the cookie over halfway through cooking. Remove from cookie sheet and cool on wire rack. Store in an airtight container for 3 weeks. Makes about 3 dozen.

BOURBON (OR RUM) BALLS

Bourbon balls based on stale cake crumbs or cookie crumbs are a tradition in my area of the South. Often they have corn syrup and cocoa added, making them more sweet and less chocolatey. The ones below are intensely bourbon and held together by semisweet chocolate. If you like bourbon balls, you'll like these best of all.

My grandmother was quite the teetotaler but she always had bourbon around for these bourbon balls and other baking. You can use extra bourbon in the bourbon-soy beef ribs on page 155.

> 3 1/2 cups crushed vanilla wafers (a 12-ounce box)
> 1 cup very finely chopped pecans
> 6 ounces semi-sweet or bittersweet chocolate
> 1/2 cup bourbon or rum
> Powdered sugar

Combine crumbs and pecans. Melt chocolate in microwave or over low heat. Stir in bourbon, little by little, stirring constantly. The chocolate will seize up and get quite thick. You can warm it a little and keep adding bourbon, it will finally relax and come together. Pour the chocolate/bourbon mixture over the crumbs and stir to mix. Form the mixture into 1-inch balls. Roll in powdered sugar. Keep 3 weeks or more in an airtight tin (they improve with time). Makes about 3 dozen.

CHOCOLATE OATMEAL BARS

Bars:
1 1/2 cups all-purpose flour
1 cup rolled oats (regular or quick-cooking)
1 cup firmly packed brown sugar
3/4 cup softened butter
1/2 teaspoon baking soda
1/2 teaspoon salt

Chocolate filling:
1 cup semi-sweet morsels
1/2 cup chopped pecans, optional

Heat oven to 350 degrees. In a large bowl, combine flour, oats, sugar, butter, soda and salt and use an electric mixer or pastry blender to mix until crumbly. Reserve 1 cup of the crumb mixture. Press the remaining in the bottom of a lightly-greased 9- by 13-inch baking pan or similar baking pan. Bake 15 minutes.

Remove from the oven and sprinkle with chocolate morsels. Allow them to stand 3 minutes, then spread them smooth. Sprinkle with pecans and press lightly. Crumble reserved crumb mixture over the top and bake 20 minutes more. Cool slightly before cutting into 24 squares.

PEPPERMINT BROWNIES

These festive brownies are good for holiday buffets.

1/2 cup butter
4 ounces unsweetened chocolate
4 eggs
2 cups sugar
1 cup all-purpose flour
1/4 teaspoon salt

Icing:
2 cups powdered sugar
3 tablespoons butter
3 ounces cream cheese
About 20 finely crushed starlight mints
1 ounce semisweet chocolate, optional

Heat oven to 350 degrees. Combine butter and chocolate and melt in a microwave or on low heat. Stir to combine and set aside to cool.

Beat eggs until slightly foamy. Continue to beat as you add sugar in a steady stream. Stir in chocolate mixture, then flour and salt. Pour batter into a 9- by 13-inch baking pan. Bake 25 minutes. Cool completely before icing.

To make the icing, beat sugar, butter and cream cheese until well-mixed. Stir in 2/3 of the crushed mints and spread on brownies. Sprinkle remaining mints on top.

If desired, melt semisweet chocolate over low heat. Scoop it into a plastic sandwich bag and squeeze it toward one corner. Clip a tiny piece of the corner off the bag and squeeze the chocolate out, drizzling it over the brownies. When the chocolate has set, cut into 40 bars.

HOLIDAY BREAKFAST

People have breakfast and brunch parties more during the holidays than any other time. Parties early in the day can be an inexpensive way to entertain and a whole lot less stressful—and you have the rest of the day to clean up.

Perhaps you just have a house full of relatives, and need to make breakfast a little more cohesive than having the kids pour their own cereal and eat while they watch television.

Below are several recipes that get you started. I don't offer alcoholic libations here, but if you're inclined to serve alcohol, it's appropriate to offer a pitcher of Mimosas or Bloody Marys.

Breakfast buffets in the summer can include melons and berries but in the winter, we rely more on citrus, pomegranates, apples, pears and dried fruits. One combination is below, but you can buy a mixture of dried fruits in a bag and simmer those until tender—add a cinnamon stick and a little sugar if you like—to keep it simple.

Then there are eggs and bread. A hot bowl of tender scrambled eggs is great. Beat them with butter flavored with minced fresh herb (chives, or rosemary). Below is a frittata recipe, which provides more flexibility than scrambled eggs because it's often served at room temperature. A cheese strata—the casserole that many brunch cooks depend on—comes with cut-out stars on the top.

For a treat, make the luscious cinnamon rolls. They take time but are soooo good. Coffee cake is simpler and nearly as delicious. (If you'd like to make a more traditional white bread, see the recipe on page 72). In lieu of baking, purchase from your favorite bakery, or provide bagels and a wide toaster.

Be sure to add some savory protein to the meal—either sliced ham, sausage, bacon or smoked salmon.

Winter Nectar
Winter Fruits Poached in White Wine
Cheddar Bread Pudding
Cheesy Herb Frittata
Cinnamon Rolls (Sticky Buns)
Sour Cream Coffee Cake

WINTER NECTAR

Fruit punches can take nearly any form. Substitute apple for pineapple juice here. Or mix grape juice, apple and cranberry. For a more festive, less sweet drink, mix the juices with seltzer or club soda.

2 cups cranberry juice cocktail
2 cups pineapple juice
2 cups orange juice
1/2 teaspoon almond extract

Combine all ingredients and serve in a glass pitcher (or other container). Serve chilled or over ice. Serves 6 to 8.

WINTER FRUITS POACHED IN WHITE WINE

In truth, any combination of fruits—fresh and dried—work in a breakfast compote. It's important to keep the mixture seasonal because that's what tastes best. Other fruits that can go into winter compote include citrus, kiwi and pomegranate seeds (kiwi contains an enzyme that breaks down other fruits, so add it at the last minute and remove it if you have leftovers).

If you prefer to use liquid other than wine, you may substitute white grape juice, but then reduce sugar to 1/4 cup, or you can use Earl Grey tea as the liquid. Sometimes the stems on dried figs can be tough – remove those that are.

1 lemon
3 cups dry white wine
3/4 cup sugar
1 cinnamon stick
4 small pears
24 dried apricots, halved
16 dried figs, halved lengthwise
1/2 cup golden raisins
1/2 cup dried cranberries or cherries
1 teaspoon vanilla
2 tablespoons rum or orange liqueur, optional

The zest is the yellow part of the lemon peel. You can remove it in long strips with a potato peeler. Combine it in a non-aluminum pan with the lemon juice, white wine, sugar, cinnamon, and 2 cups of water and bring to a boil. Reduce heat and simmer uncovered as you prepare pears. Peel pears and cut them in half lengthwise. Use a teaspoon to scoop out

(continued)

their cores. Cut them in half lengthwise. Add the pears to the liquid. Cook until barely tender, about 5 minutes. Remove pears with a slotted spoon. Add remaining ingredients to the liquid except vanilla. Simmer 10 minutes. Allow the mixture to cool, then add vanilla and pears. Refrigerate. Stir in rum or orange liqueur before serving. If you like, sprinkle pomegranate seeds over the top. Serves 16. This compote is great served with plain or vanilla yogurt and toasted nuts as a breakfast in its own right.

CHEDDAR BREAD PUDDING

Firm bread, such as Pepperidge Farm, Arnold's or Earth Grain, is best for this pudding, which tastes great when made with aged Vermont white cheddar.

The festive idea of cutting star shapes out of the bread was a chef's, not mine, but I think it's brilliant, especially for those of us not artistically inclined.

12 slices whole wheat bread
16 slices white bread
2 tablespoons Dijon mustard, or other spicy mustard
1 1/2 tablespoons Worcestershire sauce
4 large eggs, beaten lightly
1 quart whole milk
1/2 teaspoon dried thyme or 1 teaspoon fresh
1/2 teaspoon cayenne pepper
1/2 teaspoon salt
1/2 teaspoon (freshly ground) black pepper
2 cups grated extra sharp cheese (about 8 ounces)

Remove crusts from the bread. Use a 3-inch cookie cutter to cut 5 stars from the white and 5 stars from the wheat. Cut the remaining bread into approximately 2-by-2-inch squares. Toast stars in a 350-degree oven until golden, about 10 minutes. Remove from oven and turn the oven off. Transfer the bread squares to the sheet (you don't have to be real precise about this) and place in the oven to dry out.

In a bowl, stir together the mustard and Worcestershire sauce. Beat in eggs, then pour in milk as you continue to beat. Add thyme, cayenne, salt

(continued)

and pepper. Butter a 2-quart gratin or casserole dish and arrange the bread squares overlapping in it. Sprinkle with about half the cheese. Pour half the milk over and add another layer of bread. Again top with cheese and then add milk. Place stars on top, alternating colors. Cover and refrigerate overnight. Bake in a 350-degree oven for about 40 minutes or until cooked through. Serves 8.

CHEESY HERB FRITTATA

Use a non-stick skillet for this, or spray your skillet with cooking spray to ensure the easy release of eggs. Don't be real obsessive about measuring the cheese; a little more or less won't matter.

1 tablespoon olive oil or butter
8 ounces sliced mushrooms
About 1/3 cup herb cheese spread (such as Boursin, Rondele, Alouette)
10 eggs

Heat the oven to 350 degrees. Heat the olive oil or butter in a 10-inch oven-proof, non-stick skillet on medium-high heat. Tip the skillet to distribute the oil all over it. Add sliced mushrooms and cook, stirring, until they have darkened and have given up much of their juices, 5 or 10 minutes. Meanwhile, mash the cheese in a medium bowl. Add an egg and beat with cheese until well-blended (it's OK if a few lumps remain). Add the remaining eggs and beat briskly with a fork. When mushrooms are cooked, pour the beaten eggs over them. Reduce heat to medium. As the eggs become firm, use a knife or thin spatula to lift the sides away from the edges of the pan. Tip the skillet to allow uncooked eggs to flow under firmer eggs. When the eggs are nearly firm on top, put the skillet in the oven for 2 minutes, or until eggs are totally firm. Cut in wedges and serve from skillet or loosen the eggs and flip them upside down onto a plate. You may cut this in wedges or in squares and serve either hot or room temperature. Serves 8 as part of a larger breakfast.

CINNAMON ROLLS

There's nothing like good cinnamon rolls, warm out of the oven. They start with yeast dough, which intimidates some cooks. But this dough is smooth and glossy and easy to work with.

This is a great recipe to bear as a hostess gift—something you can spend time on if you're not entertaining to present to someone who is. It makes a lot, so you can keep a pan for yourself.

Rolls:
1 cup warm water
2 packages quick-rise yeast
2 eggs
1/2 cup softened butter
1/2 cup vegetable shortening
1 teaspoon salt
1 cup sugar
1 cup boiling water
8 cups flour

Cinnamon:
1/2 cup melted butter, more or less
2 cups brown sugar
4 teaspoons cinnamon

Glaze:
3 cups powdered sugar
4 tablespoons water
3 tablespoons light corn syrup
1 1/2 teaspoons vanilla
Dash salt

To make the rolls: Combine the yeast with 1 cup warm tap water, stir until the yeast dissolves. Set aside.

Beat the eggs with an electric mixer until frothy—a minute or two. In another bowl, beat the butter, shortening, salt and sugar on medium speed until the mixture is creamy, about 2 minutes. Use low speed to beat in boiling water. Add eggs and beat to blend. Add yeast and stir.

Add 2 cups flour to the egg mixture. Beat with mixer until blended. Add 2 more cups and beat a minute or so. Add 2 more cups and use a wooden spoon to mix. Add remaining flour and stir with a wooden spoon until the flour is mixed in. Remove dough from bowl and place on a lightly floured surface. Knead until smooth, 2 to 3 minutes.

Grease a large clean bowl. Place dough in bowl and turn it to grease all sides. Cover tightly with plastic wrap and set aside in a warm place until the dough has doubled in bulk, about 2 hours. Punch dough down. Divide into 2 equal portions. Roll each portion of dough into a rectangle about 12- by 16- by 1/2-inch thick.

Brush each half of dough liberally with the 1/2 cup melted butter. Combine brown sugar and cinnamon. Sprinkle over melted butter. Roll up from the short side as you would a jelly roll to create a spiral of cinnamon on the inside. The roll should be 12 inches long. Cut into 1-inch-thick slices (see note).

Grease the bottom and sides of two 9- by 13- by 2-inch pans. Place the rolls spiral side down and barely touching each other. Brush outside edge of rolls with melted butter. Cover loosely with a clean cloth and set aside in a warm place until rolls have doubled in size, about 45 minutes.

(continued)

Heat oven to 375 degrees. Place the rolls in the oven and cook 15 minutes. Remove from oven and cool 5 minutes. The rolls will look blond. If you cook them until they are brown from your perspective they will be burned on the bottom. Resist the temptation to cook them 5 more minutes. Cut around the sides of the rolls to loosen them from the sides of the pan. When they've cooled 5 minutes, turn them onto a serving tray or flat pan. If they cool any longer they will stick to the pan.

As they are cooling, make the glaze. Combine sugar, water, corn syrup, vanilla and salt. Stir until smooth. If too thick, add water a drop at a time. Drizzle over rolls while they are warm. Makes 24 large rolls.

To cut rolls evenly: Use a long piece of dental floss. Slide it under the roll 1 inch away from the end. Bring up both ends of the floss and cross over the dough, then pull the floss through the dough to slice it. You can use a knife, but it sort of smooshes the dough.

SOUR CREAM COFFEE CAKE

Frankly, I'm not too obsessive about measuring the sour cream. I use one 8-ounce container and about half of another.

Topping:
1 1/2 cups pecans
6 tablespoons melted butter
1/4 cup white sugar
2/3 cup brown sugar
1 teaspoon cinnamon

Cake:
3 cups sifted flour
1 1/2 teaspoons baking powder
1 1/2 teaspoons baking soda
3/4 teaspoon salt
3/4 cup butter
3 eggs
1 cup sugar
1 1/2 teaspoons vanilla
12 ounces sour cream (about 1 1/3 cup)

Heat oven to 350 degrees. Grease a 9- by 13-inch baking pan. Chop pecans finely and put them in a bowl with remaining topping ingredients. Stir to mix evenly and set aside.

Combine flour, baking powder, soda, and salt in a bowl or on a piece of wax paper.

(continued)

Put butter in a bowl and beat until fluffy. Add eggs, sugar, and vanilla and beat to mix.

Add 1/3 of the flour mixture to the bowl and stir to blend. Add half the sour cream and stir to blend. Repeat, ending with flour.

Spread cake batter into prepared pan, top with pecans, sprinkling as evenly as possible. Bake 45 to 55 minutes or until cake tester comes out clean. Cool at least 10 minutes before removing from pan. Cut in 15 pieces. Some of the pecan topping will have sunk into the batter and will appear throughout the cake as you cut it—that's supposed to happen. Makes 15 large pieces.

Cooking latkes

HANUKKAH

Hanukkah, the Jewish Festival of Lights, is a celebration of freedom, of a time more than 2,000 years ago when Jews drove the Syrian army out of Jerusalem and restored their own faith and culture.

The Syrian king had prevented Jews from worshiping. When the Jews recaptured the temple, they found their holy lamps had only enough oil to burn for one day, yet miraculously, they burned for eight, giving time to sanctify additional oil. The eight-day Hanukkah observance always includes telling the story and lighting an eight-branched candelabrum called a menorah. It also includes parties and sweets and lots of potato pancakes, or latkes, and is generally thought of as a food-and-fun holiday, geared toward children, with games, skits, chocolate coins and sometimes gifts. The miracle of the holy oil is celebrated in food: fried food to be specific. Potato pancakes fried in goose fat were a Russian tradition, and now these pancakes have become symbolic of Hanukkah in the United States. In Israel, jelly doughnuts are the seasonal food of choice.

Best Brisket
Lemon Honey Salmon
Latkes
Cauliflower with Breadcrumbs
Spinach with Pine Nuts
Bonnie's Winter Salad
Plum Souffle
Buttermilk Doughnuts

BEST BRISKET

Beef brisket is not just for Hanukkah, but any evening when the taste of comfort food would hit the spot. It's great for entertaining because it improves being made ahead.

2 teaspoons salt
1 teaspoon (freshly ground) pepper to taste
1 5-pound beef brisket, or chuck roast
2 fresh garlic cloves, minced, about 1 teaspoon
2 tablespoons vegetable oil
3 medium onions, peeled and diced, about 3 cups
1 14.5-ounce can crushed tomatoes
2 cups reduced-sodium beef broth or dry red wine
2 ribs celery with leaves, chopped
1 bay leaf
1 teaspoon dried thyme
1 cup chopped, fresh parsley

Heat oven to 325 degrees. Sprinkle the salt and pepper over the brisket and rub with the meat with garlic. Heat the oil in a heavy pan and sear the brisket in the oil until it is quite brown.

Put the onions in an oven proof casserole with a tight-fitting lid. Place the brisket on top of the onions fat side up. Add tomatoes, broth, celery, bay leaf, and thyme. Cover and bake 3 hours, basting occasionally.

Remove lid. Add the parsley to the liquid around the meat and bake, uncovered, for 30 minutes. The meat should be tender.

Cool the meat, then refrigerate it and gravy. When cold, skim the fat from the gravy and trim fat from the beef. Place beef on a cutting board and cut across the grain of the meat into thin slices. Refrigerate until needed.

When ready to serve, reheat the gravy. Put the sliced brisket in a roasting pan. Pour the hot gravy on the meat, cover with foil and reheat in a 350-degree oven for 30 minutes or until hot throughout.

Serve with potato pancakes or the mashed potatoes on page 38. Serves 10 or more.

LEMON HONEY SALMON

If you can't imagine latkes without sour cream, you need to make Hanukkah a fish or dairy meal. Try this salmon, or the mushroom barley soup on page 77. This is a salmon for people who love salmon, and for people who aren't sure they do. Serve it with Bonnie's salad to get flavor surprises—the sweet, tart, bitter and sour don't show up where you expect them to.

If you get an entire side of salmon that weighs three pounds, it will likely be long and thin and cook in about the time allotted. If the salmon is very large, you may get a thick, rectangular piece cut out of the middle. Cook it a little longer. In summer, try this recipe on the grill: it's fantastic.

> 3 tablespoons honey
> 3 tablespoons freshly squeezed lemon juice
> 1/2 teaspoon crushed red pepper flakes
> 2 tablespoons olive oil
> 3 cloves fresh garlic, minced
> 1 side fresh salmon, about 3 pounds, figuring 4 to 6 ounces per person
> Salt and (freshly ground) pepper, to taste
> 1 cup dry red or white wine, optional
> 2 tablespoons butter, optional

Combine honey, lemon juice, and red pepper flakes in a small bowl. Stir to mix well. Mix olive oil and garlic in a small bowl. Heat oven (or grill) to 450 degrees. Place salmon skin side down on a greased baking pan (or on the grill). Sprinkle with salt and pepper and brush with garlic oil. Cook 5 minutes, then spread with honey mixture. Bake 7 minutes more,

112

or until fish flakes easily. If the honey and juices threaten to burn in the corners of the pan, add a little water in the corners.

As you serve the fish, it should lift off the skin. Serves 8 to 10.

To make a sauce: Place the roasting pan on a burner set on high heat and immediately add 1 cup white or red wine. Stir into the corners to get any residue there, and stir as wine boils down to about 1/2 cup. Remove from heat and whip in 2 tablespoons of butter cut in 2 pieces. When the butter has melted, pour sauce over fish.

LATKES

Everyone has an opinion about how latkes should be made—small, thin and crisp all over, or fatter, with a crisp outside and tender inside. Some people add egg and flour (or matzo meal), some don't. Some people use zucchini, or apples.

I like ones made with potato, and the recipe below is the one that works the best for me. It has a little flour and lots of egg. I've made many, many different recipes, in search of ways to make them less trouble. My conclusion: good ones are trouble to make and should be served immediately, which makes them double trouble. But you will be well-loved if you go to the effort. If you must make ahead, freeze them, make them small, then reheat in a hot oven. It's not perfect, but they will be very, very good.

Remember, the oil is the point, but you can cut down on oil by using a non-stick skillet. Vegetable oil can be replaced by any fat you like, from duck or chicken fat to olive oil. This tiny bit of onion adds a respectable amount of flavor, or you can substitute a little mashed garlic, or omit it.

1 pound baking potatoes, peeled and grated
3 eggs
2 tablespoons flour
1 teaspoon salt
2 teaspoons grated onion, or to taste
1/4 cup vegetable oil

Put the grated potatoes in the middle of a clean dishtowel, gather up the sides of the towel and twist the ends to squeeze the potatoes into a

ball at the end. Twist hard to squeeze out as much excess liquid as you can.

Beat eggs in a bowl. Add potatoes, flour, salt and onion to the bowl and stir to combine. Heat a heavy (non-stick) skillet with oil in it. Make patties of potatoes in the skillet, forming them about 3 inches in diameter and 1/4 inch thick. Brown them, then turn and brown on the second side until crisp. Makes about 12.

This recipe can and probably should be doubled. If you're making a bunch of latkes, you can keep them warm on a rack over a cookie sheet in a 250-degree oven.

CAULIFLOWER WITH BREAD CRUMBS

Brown the pieces of cauliflower and toss with crunchy bread crumbs and you'll be surprised how good a humble vegetable can be.

I like making this dish with bread crumbs I've made by grinding a piece of bread in the blender. The crumbs are bigger than the ones you buy in the store, adding a little more crunch without some of the sandiness you get with store-bought crumbs. Or, if you have a supply of Japanese panko crumbs, those work admirably (and are great for coating fried fish or eggplant for Parmesan).

Add a little Parmesan cheese to the crumbs, if you like. You could also throw a few whole, peeled garlic cloves in the baking dish, if you like.

1 cauliflower, about 1 1/2 pounds, separated into large florets
Salt and (freshly ground) pepper
4 tablespoons olive oil
1/2 cup bread crumbs

Heat oven to 400 degrees. Grease a wide, shallow baking pan with 2 tablespoons olive oil. Break cauliflower into large florets. Cut cauliflower into slices about 1/2-inch thick (don't be too obsessive about this) and lay them in the pan. Sprinkle generously with salt and pepper. Mix 2 tablespoons olive oil with the bread crumbs, then sprinkle crumbs over cauliflower. Bake for 30 minutes, until the cauliflower has brown patches and the pieces have shrunk quite a bit. Serves 6.

SPINACH WITH PINE NUTS

Our supermarket sells bags of pre-washed ready-to-eat spinach. Sometimes, I buy baby leaves, which take zero time to prepare – you just dump them in a skillet. Sometimes I want the more flavorful mature leaves, which often need to have the stems pulled off and a little chopping. If pine nuts are available in your supermarket, they are likely to be near the produce. Substitute pecans if you can't find them. This dish will taste best if you mince your own garlic, rather than buying the pre-minced in a jar. In a pinch, however, that will work. The currants in this dish are nearly imperceptible. They are there to bring a barely discernible sweetness to the spinach. That's why we ask you to chop the raisins; you should be nearly unaware the fruit is there.

1/4 cup pine nuts
2 tablespoons dried currants or chopped raisins
1/3 cup olive oil
1 tablespoon (or more) minced garlic
3 10-ounce bags ready-to-eat fresh spinach
1 teaspoon salt
1/4 teaspoon hot red pepper flakes

Toast the pine nuts (or pecans) in a 350-degree oven or in a microwave until golden, about 10 minutes. Put the currants in a small cup and add enough water to cover. Set aside. Heat olive oil in a wide skillet over medium high heat. Add garlic and cook until barely golden and aromatic. Add spinach, as much as you can, and stir. As the leaves begin to collapse, add more. When all have been added, add the currants and their juice, the salt, and the red pepper flakes. Cook, stirring occasionally, for about 5 minutes. Leaves will be bright green and tender. Serve on a platter with pine nuts sprinkled over. You may also add crumbled feta cheese or a little grated Parmesan, if desired. Serves 8 to 12.

BONNIE'S WINTER SALAD

My stepmother makes a grapefruit and avocado salad that I love. It's pretty and makes a refreshing counterpoint to rich winter foods. It's appropriate for winter because that's when grapefruits are at their best.

Bonnie buys Paul Newman's olive oil and vinegar dressing to use on her salad. Use any similar dressing that appeals to you, or use the simple recipe we've provided below. Make sure the avocados are ripe and buttery, and drizzle the slices with grapefruit juice to keep them from turning brown.

The amounts of grapefruit and avocado below are approximate. You'll need to alter them depending on how your salad comes together – how big the grapefruit and avocado slices are, how much lettuce you like in proportion to the toppings, how big your plates are, etc.

**2 to 3 heads Boston lettuce (or other delicate leaf lettuce),
    approximately
3 pink grapefruits
3 ripe avocados
1/2 cup olive oil
2 tablespoons red wine vinegar, or vinegar of choice
1/2 teaspoon salt
1/2 teaspoon pepper**

Separate lettuce leaves, rinse and spin or wrap in toweling to dry the leaves (you may put the towel-enclosed leaves in a plastic bag and refrigerate them for a day or two). Peel the grapefruit and cut between the sections to create wedges. Cut the avocados in half, twist the halves and

lift apart. Smack a sharp knife into the seed and give a little twist while lifting. The seed should lift out. Cut the avocado in strips lengthwise, peeling as you do.

Combine olive oil, vinegar, salt and pepper and stir or shake to dissolve salt. Arrange dry lettuce on salad plates, then arrange grapefruit and avocados as spokes of a wheel, meeting in the middle. Drizzle with dressing and any extra grapefruit juice. Serves 8.

PLUM SOUFFLÉ

When my mother made this for us, we called it prune whip, but that doesn't quite give it the panache it deserves. It's a little trouble to make, although it was more trouble back then when she put the dried plums through a food mill to purée them and didn't have a portable mixer to beat the egg whites. But it was such a treat, and it's even better served hot with cold cream or cold custard poured over it.

1 pound dried plums or prunes (or dried fruit of choice)
5 egg whites
1/8 teaspoon salt
1/4 teaspoon cream of tartar or 1/4 teaspoon lemon juice
1/2 cup sugar

Cover prunes with water and simmer gently until soft, about 30 minutes. Cool and blend in a blender or food processor until smooth.

Lightly grease a 1 1/2 quart soufflé dish (or similar sized baking pan). Heat oven to 275 degrees. Beat egg whites, salt and cream of tartar until foamy. Sprinkle in sugar as you continue to beat. Beat egg whites until they are fluffy and form stiff peaks when you lift the beaters out. Fold in puréed plums, then scoop into prepared dish. Set the dish in a bigger pan and add hot water to come halfway up the sides. Bake for 50 to 60 minutes. Serves 6 to 8. Serve hot with cold cream or custard sauce, if desired.

POTATO DOUGHNUTS

Of course, it's not the potato that's the point of Hanukkah, it's the oil, which makes doughnuts great candidates for the observance.

They are especially appropriate if you'd like to develop a tradition that involves the children helping make something magical. This rich bread dough is easy to handle, and watching the doughnuts puff and brown in the oil borders on the fantastic. Or make them on a slow Saturday morning in February. We know a great baker who invited neighborhood children over on snow days, and they'd all make doughnuts.

The dough for these doughnuts is soft and rich. It's easy to knead and rises dramatically. If you need to stagger your cooking time, you can make the dough a day ahead of time—or even two days before—and refrigerate it well-covered, punching it down regularly. Although it won't rise quite so high and light if you keep it two days, it produces fantastic doughnuts. People who have tried these doughnuts love them, but agree that they should be served fresh and warm. We have never had leftovers.

3/4 cup mashed potatoes (instant is fine)
1/4 cup butter
2 cups buttermilk, at room temperature
1 package active dry yeast
2 tablespoons sugar
2 eggs
1 teaspoon salt
7 to 7 1/2 cups flour
About 3 cups vegetable oil
1/2 cup (or so) granulated sugar mixed with 1 teaspoon cinnamon

(continued)

While mashed potatoes are still hot, beat in butter. Stir all but 1/2 cup buttermilk into the potatoes. Sprinkle yeast and sugar into remaining buttermilk; stir to dissolve sugar. Add to potatoes. Beat eggs with salt and stir into potatoes. Beat well to remove any lumps. Add 6 cups flour to the potato mixture and stir well. Spread 1 cup of flour on a counter or other smooth surface. Turn dough onto the floured surface. Knead the dough, working the extra flour in. Knead a few minutes longer, adding a little more flour if necessary. The dough will be softer than conventional bread dough but should not be sticky. It will be easy to knead.

Place the dough in a lightly greased bowl and turn the dough to give it a lightly greased coating. Drape a cloth or plastic wrap over the bowl and set the dough aside to rise for about an hour, or until it has approximately doubled in size. Punch down with your fist, then pat or roll it to about 1/2-inch thickness. Use a 3-inch biscuit cutter or doughnut cutter to cut 3-inch circles in the dough. If you've used a biscuit cutter, you'll need a 3/4-inch round cutter (I use graduated pastry cutters that come packed in a little tin) to cut holes in the middle of the doughnuts. Pull the holes out and set them aside.

Pick up the extra dough and re-roll it and re-cut it, if desired, or roll extra dough into rounds to fry as extra doughnut holes. Let doughnuts and holes rise 30 minutes. Heat fresh, clean vegetable oil to 375 degrees. Add a few doughnuts and holes and fry until golden brown, up to 5 minutes. Turn them halfway through cooking time. (You might want to be more vigilant working with the doughnut holes, which tend to float on the browned side. Keep pushing them and turning them with a chopstick or slotted spoon until the other side browns.)

Remove them from the fat and place on absorbent toweling. As

you fry additional doughnuts, put the previously fried batch one by one into a bag or bowl of cinnamon sugar. Shake the doughnuts in the bag, or spoon the sugar over them in the bowl. Makes about 24 doughnuts. If you don't want so many doughnuts: you can make cloverleaf or other type dinner rolls. To make cloverleaves, put three 1-inch balls of dough in a greased cupcake tin and brush with a little butter. Fill any empty cupcake tins with water. Bake at 425 degrees for 15 to 18 minutes.

Stuffing potatoes

CHRISTMAS DINNER

Christmas dinner was always Christmas Eve dinner when I was growing up. It seemed to make the most sense to eat our big meal the night before we spent all day eating candy canes and chocolate and cookies.

But whether the event is Christmas Eve before or after church, or Christmas afternoon with the whole family, Christmas dinner, at least for the diners, has a magical quality about it, the glow that comes from the lights on the tree and on the table. We've spent an entire season reestablishing relationships through cards, visits, parties, and gift exchanges. Maybe it drove us crazy throughout the season, but at Christmas dinner we can reflect, and be satisfied.

For the cook, Christmas dinner is one more, perhaps one last, effort for the holidays. I rely on the handy roast—push it into the oven, pull it out of the oven. I love standing rib roast, but leg of lamb, ham, and turkey are just as easy.

Standing Rib Roast
Yorkshire Pudding
Twice-Baked Potatoes
Oyster Stew
Broccoli with Lemon Sauce
Honey Roasted Carrots
Parker House Rolls
Coconut Cake
Mocha Mousse

STANDING RIB ROAST

During the holidays, meat cutters are accustomed to taking orders for standing rib roast. They will ask you how many ribs you want, with 12 being the maximum (that's a very large roast). A 4-rib roast serves a group of 8 to 10, usually. Order from the small end of the rack, and ask the meat cutter to leave on a generous layer of fat, if you plan to make gravy and Yorkshire pudding.

It is customary for your meat cutter to remove the ribs from the meat and then tie them back together so that you may cook conventionally (with bones on) but carve more easily. If your meat cutter is not so solicitous, you'll find that this is not a difficult roast to carve with the bone on. Hang on to the bones; they make delicious eating.

Opinions differ on how best to cook the roast. I prefer to start with high heat and turn the oven down when the roast goes in. It gives the roast a browner, more delicious outer surface.

I reiterate my suggestion that you use a meat thermometer to judge the cooking time of the roast. This is an expensive piece of meat. It doesn't make sense to ruin it because you don't use a $6 tool.

1 standing rib roast
Salt
Pepper

Heat oven to 550 degrees. Salt the meat all over the surface. Place the meat fat side up on a rack in a roasting pan. Do not add any water or

cover the meat. When the oven is heated, slide the roast in, close the oven door and immediately turn heat to 350 degrees.

Roast the meat 15 minutes to the pound and then check its temperature. If you want rare meat, you'll want to remove the roast at 120 degrees – the internal temperature will rise as it stands (you want it to stand 10 to 20 minutes so that it will carve more easily). Aim to cook the meat a total of 17 minutes to the pound for medium-rare (140 degrees internally), but several factors affect how quickly the meat cooks, so be flexible.

Let the meat stand out of the oven 15 to 20 minutes before carving. Pour drippings into a large glass measuring cup or other container. You'll need the fat (it's clear and rises to the top), for gravy and Yorkshire pudding. Put the juices (the darker liquid at the bottom of the container) into the gravy.

To make beef gravy: Follow the directions for making turkey gravy on page 16, using canned reduced-sodium beef broth (or your own homemade) for the liquid.

Leftover bones: I love the meat nearest the bone and will cook the leftover rib bones in a toaster oven for up to an hour to get them crisp and brown. Renowned cookbook author James Beard described a mustard-breadcrumb mixture to spread on ribs before reheating. If you're not a rib-gnawer, consider simmering the bones in water to make a broth for mushroom barley soup (page 77).

YORKSHIRE PUDDING

This English side dish adds that Victorian-England touch to Christmas dinner. It starts off with what resembles popover batter. It comes out tasting like one huge, delicious dumpling. Cooked in a generous amount of fat in a hot oven, it should be crisp on the outside, tender—some might say doughy—on the inside.

1/2 cup beef fat or melted butter
1 1/2 cups all-purpose flour
3/4 teaspoon salt
3 eggs
1 1/2 cups milk

Heat oven to 400 degrees. Put all but 2 tablespoons of beef fat in a 9- by 13-inch size baking dish or similar size pan. Place the pan in the oven.

Combine flour and salt in a medium bowl. In another bowl, beat the eggs. Beat in milk and 2 tablespoons beef fat. Pour into flour and beat well. The mixture should be thin and smooth.

Remove the pan from the oven—the fat should be very hot—and pour the batter into it. Place back in the oven and cook 40 to 50 minutes, or until very brown around the sides. Serve immediately. Serves 10.

SARAH'S TWICE-BAKED POTATOES

Make these up to 3 months before your dinner and freeze them. Put them on a cookie sheet until they've frozen hard, then stack them in freezer containers.

12 medium potatoes
Salt and pepper
6 tablespoons butter
2 cloves fresh garlic, minced (about 1 teaspoon)
1 1/2 cups milk, preferably whole
1/4 to 1/2 cup freshly grated Parmesan or Romano cheese

Heat oven to 400 degrees. Wash potatoes well to remove all grit from skin. Prick potatoes with a fork and place them in the oven. Bake 60 minutes or until tender. Remove from oven and, holding the potato in one hand (line your hand first with a pot holder), use a sharp knife to cut about 1/2 inch off the long side of the potato, to make a little boat. Scrape any potato off the skin you've removed and put it into a bowl. Throw that little piece of skin away. Scoop the potato meat out of the large piece into the bowl, leaving 1/4 to 1/2 inch of potato inside the skin. Repeat with remaining potatoes. Melt butter in a small saucepan. Add garlic and cook over medium heat just a minute or two, until it is aromatic. Remove and discard garlic. Put the potato through a ricer or food mill, add garlic butter, milk and salt and pepper and beat with a spoon to blend (alternatively, combine butter, milk, salt and pepper with potato and beat with a mixer to blend). Stuff mashed potatoes back into potato-skin boats and sprinkle the top with grated cheese. Refrigerate or freeze until needed. If cold, bake 1 hour at 350 degrees to reheat. If frozen, heat 1 hour at 400 degrees to reheat. Serves 12.

OYSTER STEW

Oyster stew is not really a stew, as it is barely cooked. The oysters are heated only until the edges curl. That way the oysters stay tender. It is typically served as its own course in wide bowls.

1 cup milk
1 cup light cream
2 cups fresh oysters
2 tablespoons lightly salted butter
Salt and cayenne pepper, to taste
Paprika
Oyster crackers or French bread (optional)

Heat the milk and cream together until very hot, but do not allow to boil. Add the oysters, butter and salt. When the butter melts, remove the stew from direct heat. Place over or in a larger pan of simmering water. Allow the stew to ripen a few minutes, stirring it gently. Taste for salt. Ladle a small amount (it is very rich) into bowls and sprinkle with a little paprika. Pass the Tabasco and fresh, crisp oyster crackers or French bread. Serves 8.

BROCCOLI WITH LEMON SAUCE

My mother made this sauce always on Christmas and other special occasions. She called it hollandaise, but it is nothing like real hollandaise. This is much more stable and easier to cook. I'm not sure I've ever seen it curdle. It is very lemony. Leftover egg whites may be used in the coconut cake at the end of this chapter or the plum souffle on page 120.

1 head broccoli
1/3 cup fresh lemon juice
1/3 cup butter, cut into pieces
3 egg yolks
1/2 teaspoon salt

Remove the tough stems of the broccoli and cut the broccoli head into bite-size florets. Cook the broccoli in the microwave, steamer or boiling water until it is bright green and barely tender. (I cook mine by submerging the florets in a pan of boiling, salted water and cooking, uncovered, 5 minutes, but I am not as adept at microwaving vegetables as other cooks are.)

Meanwhile, combine the lemon juice, butter, egg yolks and salt in a small bowl and set it over a pan of hot water. Heat the water until it simmers, stirring the mixture as the water heats and the butter begins to melt. Keep stirring to blend the ingredients, which will begin to thicken as they heat through. When the mixture is thick, remove from heat. Stir in a tablespoon or two of the hot water from the pan to loosen it up a little. Serve over hot broccoli. This dish serves 6 people. The recipe doubles easily. You can keep the sauce warm over the hot water for a little while, though you may need to loosen it again with a little hot water.

OVEN ROASTED CARROTS WITH HONEY AND PEPPER

Honey and pepper is a magical flavor combination, and you don't need too much of either to bring out the best in roasted carrots. The secret to this dish is getting the carrots distinctly brown on at least one side. If you have kosher salt, use it for the carrots, and increase the amount to 3/4 teaspoon.

1 1/2 pounds baby carrots (substitute, peeled, large carrots cut up)
1/4 cup butter
1 teaspoon (freshly ground) black pepper
1/2 teaspoon salt, or to taste
2 tablespoons honey

Heat oven to 400 degrees. Cut the butter into 3 or 4 pieces and place on a wide, shallow baking sheet. Put in the oven to melt the butter, then tip the pan so that it coats the bottom. Scatter carrots over the pan. Sprinkle with salt and pepper. Bake 20 minutes, stirring once, until the carrots are beginning to brown. Drizzle with honey and bake 10 minutes more. Serves 8.

PARKER HOUSE ROLLS

Not every cook feels confident about making yeast rolls, but they really aren't difficult and certainly do make dinner special. Roll-making can adapt to your schedule—make the dough the night before you need them rolls and refrigerate (cover the bowl with plastic wrap). The dough will have risen perfectly by morning.

Most dinner roll doughs resemble each other; some are sweeter, some more tender. The shape is what makes a Parker House roll (made famous by the Parker House dining room, in Boston). If you'd like a change of pace, roll the dough into walnut-sized balls, put three in a muffin tin, brush with butter and bake. Serve them as "cloverleaf" rolls.

2 cups milk
1/4 cup butter
2 tablespoons sugar
2 teaspoons salt
2 packages active dry yeast (about 1 1/2 teaspoons)
5 to 6 cups all-purpose flour
Melted butter

Place the milk, butter, sugar and salt in a small saucepan and heat over medium heat, stirring to dissolve the sugar and salt. When the butter is melted, remove from heat. Combine the yeast with 1/4 cup warm water in a small bowl and stir to blend.

Put 4 cups of flour in a large bowl. When the milk has cooled to lukewarm, add it and the yeast to the flour. Stir to blend. Add enough remaining flour to make a soft dough.

(continued)

Spread a little flour on a clean counter top and flatten the dough out with the heels of your hands. Fold the dough over, turn it a quarter turn, flatten and fold again. Keep flattening and folding until the dough is smooth, adding a little flour as necessary to keep the dough from sticking. Place in a lightly greased bowl, brush the top with melted butter, cover the bowl with plastic wrap and allow the mixture to rise until doubled in bulk, about 1 1/2 hours at room temperature (or overnight in the fridge).

Punch dough down, smooth the surface, brush with butter, cover the bowl with plastic wrap and allow the mixture to rise until doubled in bulk, about 1 hour at room temperature (or overnight in the fridge).

Turn the dough onto a lightly floured counter and press out to smooth and flatten. Roll it to about 1/2 inch thick. Brush with butter. Use a sharp knife to cut the dough in 2- by 3-inch (or so) strips. Fold the rectangle the long way, so that the top half is just shy of the bottom half. Place the shorter side down on a generously greased baking sheet with shallow sides. Brush top with butter. Repeat with the next roll, placing it slightly over the first one, to make long, vertical rows of overlapping rolls. Place the next row close but not touching the first, and build another row. Cover with a clean dish towel or plastic wrap and set aside for 30 minutes. Heat oven to 375 degrees. Bake rolls for 10 to 15 minutes, until the rolls are golden brown. Brush with more melted butter when they come out of the oven. Makes about 3 dozen rolls.

BLUE RIBBON COCONUT CAKE

This cake won a blue ribbon in the Kentucky State Fair years ago and it has been my standard coconut cake ever since. The icing is different from the normal butter/powdered sugar mixture, though that will work if you prefer it (follow the recipe on your bag or box of powdered sugar). White Lily flour is milled in Tennessee and makes very tender cakes and biscuits. If you can't find it, substitute cake flour.

Cake:
1 cup butter (room temperature)
2 cups sugar
3 cups White Lily flour (sift before measuring)
3 teaspoons baking powder
1 cup whole milk
6 egg whites
1 1/2 teaspoons vanilla
1/4 teaspoon almond extract

Frosting:
5 tablespoons flour
1 cup whole milk
1/2 cup butter
1/2 cup vegetable shortening
1 cup sugar
2 teaspoons vanilla
8 ounces flaked coconut

Grease and flour two 9-inch round cake pans. Heat oven to 350 degrees.

(continued)

To make the cake: Beat butter and sugar until mixed. Sift flour and baking powder together twice, and add to butter mixture alternately with milk, stirring with a spoon to mix. Beat egg whites until stiff but not dry. Fold into flour mixture and add vanilla and almond flavorings. Pour into cake pans and bake on the middle rack of the oven for 30 to 35 minutes, or until cake has browned and springs back when lightly pressed with your finger. Turn onto wire cake racks to cool.

To make the frosting: Put flour into a small saucepan. Gradually add milk, stirring until smooth. Cook over medium-low heat, stirring until mixture is thick. Remove from heat and cool to room temperature. Do not refrigerate. Beat together butter and shortening with an electric mixer. Add 1 cup sugar gradually while continuing to beat. Add vanilla and beat for 5 minutes. Add cooled milk mixture and continue to beat for another 5 minutes. Frost bottom layer of cake with a quarter of the frosting. Place top layer on this and frost it and sides with remaining frosting. Pat coconut on sides of cake. Sprinkle remaining coconut on top of cake until all is used. Place in cake saver, if possible. Serves 12.

Note on keeping cake: Do not put foil or plastic wrap on this frosting. It will adhere to both. To keep cake fresh, put foil against the cut sides of the cake.

MOCHA MOUSSE

The Kahlua does not give this creamy mousse a particularly alcoholic taste, but if you want to avoid the alcohol altogether, substitute strong coffee or simply add more hot cream

2 1/2 cups heavy (whipping) cream, see note
12 ounces semi-sweet chocolate, morsels or chopped small
1/4 cup Kahlua, coffee or flavoring liquid of choice
1 Heath bar (or other chocolate toffee)

Heat 1 1/2 cups cream in the microwave or on top of the stove until just boiling.

Put the chocolate chips in a blender. When the cream is hot, pour it into the blender through the hole in the lid while blending chips. Pour slowly and keep blending until all the cream is added. Add Kahlua and keep blending. You may need to scrape down the sides a few times to blend evenly. When the mixture is smooth, pour the contents into 8 wine glasses or other decorative dessert containers. Chill.

Before serving, whip 1 cup of cream. Top mousse with cream and sprinkle with finely chopped Heath bar. Serves 8.

Homemade whipped cream: Place 1 cup cream in a small but deep bowl and beat with an electric mixer, slowly at first, until it thickens and becomes fluffy. You may want to sweeten it with a tablespoon of sugar, but this chocolate is very rich, and the unsweetened cream is a nice contrast.

Mussels in skillet

NEW YEAR'S EVE COCKTAIL PARTY

Despite the fact that New Year's Eve is the biggest video rental night of the year, there are people who prefer to celebrate the coming new year with appropriate enthusiasm. Even if you do rent a movie on December 31 and watch the ball drop from the privacy of your TV room, you may be organizing a cocktail party at some point in your life. This menu fills the bill.

The stress of hors d'oeuvres comes from fiddling with little tiny pieces of food geared to feed grown-ups. How do you pull it off? And how do you plan?

I like to serve foods that are prepared in big amounts, but end up being individual pieces, like quiches and frittatas that you cook in big pans and cut in small squares (see the frittata on page 101). It doesn't require as much dexterity as wrapping a snow pea around a shrimp. Cut chicken breasts into strips, marinate them in vinegar, oil and an herb and skewer them for grilling or broiling. Cut feta cheese into small squares and skewer with a cherry tomato half and black olive, or use mozzarella and a basil leaf with the tomato.

Champagne Punch
Spicy Almonds
Tenderloin Toasts with Blue Cheese
Artichoke Bites
Mussels Vinaigrette
Wasabi Cucumbers
Tuxedo Cakes

When you're planning, consider these tips:

• If you'd like a certain amount of fussy, labor-intensive hors d'oeuvres, hire a catering company to produce a recipe or two, or hire a teenager to come to the house and assemble them. That teenager could stay through the evening, picking up empty plates and wine glasses and refilling trays.

• If the cocktail party replaces a meal, serve a selection of hearty hors d'oeuvres—meaty or cheesy. If it replaces a dinner meal, plan at least 14 pieces per person.

• Add variety to the table by serving dips in food containers—a radicchio cup, hollowed bell pepper, hollowed melon, hollowed out tomato etc.

• For other appetizer ideas, check the short ribs on page 155, the pita crisps on page 156 and the spice rubbed Baltimore-style beef roast on page 67.

• One guest will likely eat 6 pieces the first hour and 4 every hour thereafter. Double those numbers if you serve shrimp.

CHAMPAGNE PUNCH

2 tablespoons sugar
1 cup cognac
Dash bitters
3 (750 ml) bottles champagne

Stir sugar into cognac until dissolved. Shake in some bitters. Put a scant tablespoon of the cognac mixture into each glass and top with cold champagne. Serves 20.

SPICY ALMONDS

These nuts are good for snacking and chopped on top of green salads or vegetables.

2 cups blanched almonds
2 tablespoons melted butter
1 tablespoon sugar
1/2 teaspoon cumin
1/2 teaspoon chili powder
1/2 teaspoon cayenne pepper
1/2 teaspoon salt

Heat oven to 325 degrees. Put the almonds in a bowl. Drizzle with butter and stir to coat. Combine sugar, cumin, chili powder, cayenne and salt in a small cup and sprinkle it over the almonds, tossing to coat evenly. Spread on a baking sheet and bake 20 to 25 minutes, stirring occasionally, until the nuts are aromatic and have browned. Remove from oven and remove nuts from baking sheet to cool before serving. Cool completely before storing.

TENDERLOIN TOASTS WITH BLUE CHEESE

Whether you're serving appetizers at a cocktail party or a sit-down dinner for 12, this boneless, easy-to-carve, tender meat earns high honors as party food. I reviewed the basics of beef tenderloin in my book, *Derby 101*, but I repeat them here.

• Whole beef tenderloin sold either trimmed or untrimmed, weighs from 4 to 7 pounds.

• Trimmed meat has had all fat and silverskin removed (silverskin is an inedible, tough membrane that can be removed from the meat with a sharp knife).

• Supermarket chains often feature special prices on whole, untrimmed beef tenderloin. It comes in a transparent, oxygen-free wrapper and the implication is that you will trim the meat yourself. Save yourself time and ask the meat cutter to trim it for you.

• If you end up trimming it, remove the thin outer membrane, the tough silverskin and fat deposits on the outside of the meat, including fat that runs the length of the tenderloin. Remove these fat deposits, and you'll have some loose, thin side pieces of meat flapping off the main roast, which need to be tied to the main part of the roast.

• You'll know you have a wonderful butcher if he ties the tenderloin together so it looks neat and cooks evenly. If the piece you buy seems to have a bigger middle and one or two loose sides, you may want to ask the meat cutter to tie it for you. Or you can tie it yourself at home. Even a crude tying with cotton string will help the meat cook more evenly and make it more attractive than letting the flaps hang loose. It doesn't need to look perfect when you tie it.

Even "inexpensive" beef tenderloin is an expensive cut, so you don't

want to overcook it. Now may be the time to buy a meat thermometer from your favorite cookware store, department store or supermarket, and use it. Because the beef tenderloin has no fat marbling to speak of, it will be extremely tough and dried out if you cook it all the way through. If you want to prepare meat to the well-done stage, it's best to choose a less expensive meat, such as sirloin tip. Beef tenderloin tapers at one end. The ''butt end,'' or widest part, can be rare while the tail end is less so. If you want the whole roast to cook evenly, turn the thin end under and tie it so the roast has a uniform thickness.

Using a meat thermometer is the best way to ensure the meat is cooked to the desired doneness. In a pinch, you can cut into the meat to check its color.

2 1/2 to 3 pounds beef tenderloin
1 tablespoon olive oil
1 teaspoon salt
1/2 teaspoon (freshly ground) black pepper

Blue cheese spread:
1 cup (4 ounces) blue cheese
8 ounces sour cream
1 cup mayonnaise
1 teaspoon Worcestershire sauce
1 teaspoon hot sauce

2 1-pound French bread loaves
Softened butter
Fresh chives, optional

(continued)

Remove the meat from the refrigerator an hour before cooking.

Heat the oven to 500 degrees. Brush the meat with olive oil. Sprinkle with salt and pepper. Place on a roasting pan, put the pan in the oven, shut the door and immediately reduce heat to 400 degrees. Roast the beef 30 minutes and read its internal temperature. At 125 degrees, its center will be red and slightly warm. At 135, the center will be pink. Remove from oven, drape loosely with a piece of foil and let the meat stand at least 10 minutes before trying to carve it. (Its internal temperature will rise a few degrees on standing.) It will slice most easily if you let it cool completely.

Mix blue cheese, sour cream, mayonnaise, Worcestershire and hot sauce. Refrigerate.

Slice baguettes about 1/4-inch thick on the diagonal. Spread on a cookie sheet and bake in a 350-degree oven for 10 minutes until dry but not colored. Remove and cool. Spread each with butter, top with a thin slice of meat—try to cover the toast completely. Top with a dollop of blue cheese mix. Top with a garnish of chive, if desired.

To assemble early: Spread baguette pieces with butter and top with beef. Place a layer of toasts on a tray, cover with plastic wrap and put on another layer. Refrigerate up to a day. Dollop with blue cheese and decorate with chives just before serving.

ARTICHOKE BITES

This is a frittata of sorts, easy and delicious.

4 eggs
2 6-ounce jars marinated artichoke hearts
1 clove garlic, about 1/2 teaspoon minced
1 cup grated cheddar cheese
1 teaspoon Worcestershire
1/4 teaspoon Tabasco
1/2 cup crumbled saltine crackers

Heat oven to 325 degrees. Spray an 8- by 8-inch pan with nonstick spray.

Beat eggs in a medium sized bowl. Coarsely chop artichoke hearts and place in the bowl with their marinade. Mince garlic and add it. Add remaining ingredients. Pour into pan and bake 35 to 40 minutes. Cool completely before cutting into small squares. Makes 25.

WASABI CUCUMBERS

Wasabi is the nose-clearing green horseradish of Japanese sushi bars. Some supermarkets carry wasabi powder or the paste in tubes. Mixing it with sour cream cools a little of the fire, which comes on strong but disappears quickly, making it quite addictive. Garnish these cucumbers with pickled ginger and you get a burst of the best of Japanese flavors.

3 cucumbers
8 ounces sour cream
1 teaspoon wasabi powder, or to taste
Pickled ginger

If you'd like to serve the cucumbers peeled, you can peel them first, or cut the cucumber in slices and use a scalloped-edged round cutter to cut the skins away and create an attractive edge on the cucumber.

Cut the cucumber into thin rounds, about 1/4-inch thick. Mix sour cream and wasabi paste. Place a dab of wasabi cream on each cucumber round and garnish with a slice of pickled ginger. Makes about 70 slices.

MUSSELS VINAIGRETTE

If you are not familiar with the New Zealand green mussels frozen on the half shell, run, don't walk, to your favorite seafood store or well-stocked supermarket and buy some. They are clean and grit free, and are as plump as clams; delicious and work-free.

This mussel recipe came from a Spanish chef who serves them as tapas (hence the use of sherry vinegar). They are very pretty on a buffet, and could not be easier or more delicious. Just the clean, fresh taste you like after a season of rich food.

2 pounds New Zealand green mussels or 2 dozen mussels
1 thick lemon slice
1/2 cup olive oil
3 tablespoons sherry vinegar or other vinegar
Salt and pepper
1 tablespoon finely minced onion
1/2 green pepper, finely minced
1/2 red pepper, finely minced

If using fresh mussels, scrub them. Put mussels in a wide skillet with lemon slice. Add 1 cup water, bring to a boil, cover and lower heat to steam mussels open. Remove open ones from the skillet and discard any that don't open. For the New Zealand mussels, steam about 7 minutes. Take the tops off mussels (New Zealand have no tops). Put them on a wide serving tray and chill.

Combine olive oil, vinegar, salt, and pepper and whisk to blend. Add onion and peppers. Spoon over mussels and refrigerate until serving. Serves 8 to 10 as appetizers.

TUXEDO CAKES

Cake layer:
14 ounces bittersweet or semisweet chocolate
10 tablespoons butter
3/4 cup sugar
5 eggs
1/2 cup flour

Truffle topping:
2/3 cup heavy (whipping) cream
6 ounces bittersweet or semisweet chocolate, morsels or chopped

Line a 9- by 13-inch baking pan with aluminum foil, pressing it into the corners and allowing the foil to overhang the ends. Spray the foil with cooking spray.

To make the cake: combine chocolate and butter in a pan or bowl and heat over low heat on the stove or in the microwave until the chocolate is melted, stirring occasionally. Set aside to cool.

Heat oven to 350 degrees. When the chocolate has cooled, beat eggs until foamy. Add sugar gradually as you continue to beat. Stir in chocolate mixture, then flour. Pour into prepared pan and bake 20 minutes, until firm to the touch. Cool completely.

To make the truffle topping: combine cream and chocolate in a small bowl and heat in microwave on medium power or set in a little hot water, stirring occasionally, until chocolate is melted and they are blended. Cool completely.

Use a 2-inch biscuit cutter to cut 24 rounds out of the cake layer. Place the rounds on a rack and spoon truffle topping over cakes, letting it glaze the top and drip down the sides. Allow to stand at room temperature until the icing firms a little. These are classic as is, but if you'd like to decorate, add a chip of peppermint candy, a little candied orange rind, etc.

To use leftover crumbs: Crumble into a bowl. Soak with bourbon. Add toasted pecans. Press into balls, roll in powdered sugar.

Tiramisu

NEW YEAR'S DAY OPEN HOUSE

Everybody in the South expects to have black-eyed peas and greens for New Year's Day. They're good luck—the beans represent coins, the greens, folding money. Even if the superstition of good fortune doesn't hold true, the reality of good health will. These foods are powerfully good for you, and there's no better time to eat them than when you're starting over for the New Year.

Lucky Black-Eyed Peas
Black-Eyed Pea Salsa
Thick Kale Stew
Bourbon-Soy Short Ribs
Pita Crisps
Tiramisu

LUCKY BLACK-EYED PEAS

This vegetarian dish relies on dried tomatoes for a meaty richness. Many gardeners have found themselves drying excess tomatoes in the summer, others find the tomatoes packed in oil in specialty food stores, or in clear pouches with other specialty foods at their supermarket. Any of these products will work here. It's the concentrated flavor that you're looking for. Cut the tomatoes in small pieces.

3 cups dried black-eyed peas (1 pound)
1 medium onion
1 red bell pepper (green may substitute)
4 to 5 large cloves garlic
3 tablespoons olive oil
1/2 cup dried tomatoes
1/2 teaspoon black pepper
1/2 teaspoon crushed red pepper, or to taste
2 teaspoons basil
1 teaspoon oregano
1/2 teaspoon thyme
1 teaspoon salt, or more to taste

Soak black-eyed peas overnight in water to cover. Peel and mince the onion. Core, seed and dice the pepper. Peel and mince garlic. Heat olive oil in a 4 1/2-quart pot and add onion, pepper and garlic. Cook about 15 minutes over medium heat, stirring occasionally, until vegetables are limp. Meanwhile, chop dried tomatoes. Add to pot along with peas, black and red peppers, basil, oregano, thyme, salt and 2 quarts water. Cover and simmer 2 hours. Serves 6 to 8. Serve with pita crisps or cornbread.

BLACK-EYED PEA SALSA

Rather than serving a large pot of cooked black-eyed peas, perhaps a more piquant salsa would appeal. This makes a great counterpoint to the thick kale stew.

3 cups cooked black-eyed peas
1 cup diced red onion
1/2 cup chopped, fresh cilantro
1/2 cup diced celery
1/2 cup peeled and diced cucumber
1/4 cup fresh lemon juice, or to taste
Salt and (freshly ground) pepper to taste

Combine all ingredients in a bowl. Serve as a side dish with soup.

THICK KALE STEW

This is a hall-of-fame recipe, one that pleases nearly all the people all the time, even the skeptics. Any culture that relies on pork and greens has some combination like this one. I've used all manner of flavorful meats for this, from ham hock to link sausage to breakfast sausage. I like it when the potatoes get way over-cooked and fall apart to thicken the broth. This soup improves on standing. Cook it a day or two before you need it and reheat. It also freezes beautifully. I don't peel the potatoes, but you can if you like. You are not going to believe how delicious this stew is.

> 3 tablespoons olive oil or vegetable oil
> 1/2 pound smoked sausage or ham
> 1 large onion
> 6 to 8 large cloves garlic
> 4 large potatoes
> 1 large bunch kale
> 2 quarts water, or substitute some chicken stock
> 2 16-ounce cans white beans
> Salt and lots of (freshly ground) black pepper

Heat olive oil in a wide, deep soup pot over medium heat. Add sausage or ham, chopping it into small pieces. Dice onion and add it to pan. Mince garlic and add it. Cook them together, stirring often, until they soften, about 5 or 10 minutes. Meanwhile, dice potatoes. Wash and stem kale and slice in slivers. Add potatoes and kale to the pot as you prepare them. Add water. Increase heat to high and bring stew to a boil. Reduce heat, simmer 20 to 25 minutes or until potatoes are very soft. Use a potato masher or fork to roughly mash the potatoes and thicken the broth. Add beans and heat through. Season with salt and pepper. Serves 6 to 8. Serve with large of hunks of rustic bread, or corn bread, or pita crisps.

BOURBON-SOY SHORT RIBS

I make these as finger-food. There isn't a lot of meat to them, but they're a blast to nosh on. Let the soup and beans fill people up, and let these ribs give them a burst of flavor. In my market, beef short ribs come already cut in 3- and 4-inch lengths. Oh, and pass the napkins.

Can you omit the bourbon? Well, yes. But you can also consider it just another concentrated flavor like the sesame oil and soy sauce. There's certainly no alcohol left after all the cooking.

1/3 cup sugar
1/3 cup water
1/3 cup soy sauce
3 tablespoons bourbon
2 tablespoons Asian sesame oil
1 small onion, cut into chunks
1 inch fresh ginger, peeled and roughly chopped
1 clove garlic
6 pounds lean, well-trimmed beef short ribs, cut into 3- to 4-inch
    lengths

Combine in blender: sugar, water, soy sauce, bourbon, oil, onion, ginger and garlic. Blend until smooth. Put ribs in ''zipper style'' plastic bags (it might take 2) and pour marinade over ribs. Seal bags, turn them over a couple of times to distribute marinade among ribs and refrigerate. (Put the bag on a plate in case it leaks.) Refrigerate 4 hours, overnight, or a day or two, turning bag occasionally. Bake on rack in a shallow roasting pan and cook at 325 degrees for 1 1/2 hours. You may also cook them over indirect heat on the charcoal or gas grill for an incredible grill flavor. Serves 10 if there's lots of other food around. Serves 6 as an entrée.

PITA CRISPS

The kosher salt and freshly ground pepper make these crisps taste better than you'd think they could. If you don't have a pepper grinder, buy the pepper in a jar that has the grinder attached. For this recipe, it makes a big difference.

1/3 cup olive oil
1 clove garlic, peeled and pressed flat with the side of a knife
6 pita breads, about 6 inches in diameter
Coarse salt, such as kosher
Freshly ground pepper
Parmesan cheese, optional

Heat oven to 400 degrees. Combine olive oil and garlic. Split 6 pita breads into 12 rounds. Brush the insides of the rounds with oil, sprinkle with salt and grind pepper over the top. Sprinkle with a little Parmesan cheese, if desired. Place on 2 or 3 large baking sheets and bake (in shifts if necessary) 5 to 10 minutes, or until brown and crisp. Cut or break into pieces and serve in a bread basket. Serves 8 or so.

TIRAMISU

Tiramisu is the little "pick-me-up" dessert of Italy with one of the richest cream cheeses—mascarpone—and flavors of Cognac and coffee. It is similar to trifle and other desserts that combine dry cake with wet flavorings and custardy fillings. Traditionally tiramisu was made with raw egg yolks. Here's a recipe that isn't.

Mascarpone is much richer and softer than cream cheese and makes the dish distinctive. You can find it at specialty markets. Ladyfingers are low-fat cake cooked in oblong shapes, good for breaking apart and shaping the way you need them. Some that you buy are very moist, others are dry. Just change the amount of cold coffee you pour over them, or whip a little more cream for folding into the mascarpone, if yours are on the dry side.

The following quantities are somewhat approximate—mascarpone is usually found in 8- and 16-ounce containers so that's a good number to start with. Depending on what serving dish I'm using, I may use more or fewer ladyfingers and chocolate. A little tiramisu goes a long way—it's very rich. If you'd like to serve more than 8 people, make additional ones, rather than bigger ones, so you'll maintain the correct proportion of cake to filling. The alcohol flavor is characteristic of tiramisu but it is not strong. If you object to using it, substitute more coffee in the mascarpone mixture, and add a little more sugar.

This is a good make-ahead dish. It doesn't come into its own until it has ripened overnight.

(continued)

TIRAMISU

16 ounces mascarpone cheese, at room temperature
1/3 cup sugar
3 tablespoons coffee liqueur, such as Kahlua
3 tablespoons cognac
1 teaspoon vanilla
1 1/2 cups heavy (whipping) cream
24 ladyfingers
1 cup cold espresso or strong coffee
4 ounces semisweet chocolate, very finely chopped or grated

Combine mascarpone, sugar, coffee liqueur, cognac and vanilla in a bowl and beat to blend completely.

In a small, chilled bowl, beat cream until stiff peaks form. Fold 2/3 of the whipped cream into the mascarpone mixture.

Cover the bottom of a 1 1/2 quart souffle dish or other container with ladyfingers. Drizzle with cold coffee. Cover with half the mascarpone and grate half the chocolate over it. Repeat. The top layer should be chocolate. Garnish with whipped cream. Refrigerate several hours or overnight. Serves 8 or more.

Make 12 individual servings by creating the layers in individual serving dishes (stemware is pretty, either sherbet dishes or wine glasses).

INDEX